JAMES BAILEY is a writer who was born in Bristol but now calls different places home, working nomadically from cities such as Florence, Vienna and New York. His novels *The Flip Side* and *The Way Back to You* have both been translated into multiple languages. Before becoming an author, James worked as a red carpet reporter and a tour guide, and even carried the 2012 Olympic Torch.

Find out more about James on www.JamesBaileyWrites.com
or on Instagram @JamesBaileyWrites.

The
Meaning
of Life

Letters from Extraordinary People and their
Answer to Life's Biggest Question

James Bailey

ROBINSON

ROBINSON
First published in Great Britain in 2025 by Robinson
3 5 7 9 10 8 6 4 2

A CIP catalogue record for this book is available from the British Library.

ISBN: 978-1-47214-967-1 (hardcover)
ISBN: 978-1-47214-968-8 (trade paperback)

Design by Clare Sivell
Typeset in Adobe Garamond and Mencken Std
Printed and bound in Great Britain by Clays Ltd, Elcograf S.p.A.
Papers used by Robinson are from well-managed forests and other responsible sources.

Robinson
An imprint of
Little, Brown Book Group
Carmelite House
50 Victoria Embankment
London EC4Y 0DZ

The authorised representative
in the EEA is
Hachette Ireland
8 Castlecourt Centre, Dublin 15,
D15 XTP3, Ireland
(email: info@hbgi.ie)

An Hachette UK Company
www.hachette.co.uk
www.littlebrown.co.uk

Contents

SURVIVORS AND CAMPAIGNERS 138

ATHLETES AND ADVENTURERS 184

THINKERS, PHILOSOPHERS AND FUTURISTS   342

Introduction

IN SEPTEMBER 2015, I was unemployed, heartbroken and living alone in my dead grandad's caravan, wondering what the meaning of life was.

It's fair to say it wasn't what I thought I'd be doing shortly before turning twenty-four years old.

By this age I'd envisaged that I'd be starting some high-flying job, earnings lots of money and enjoying the start of adulthood. Yet, having graduated from university with little to show for the experience apart from a piece of paper and mountains of debt, I was lost. Completely and utterly lost.

People say that your university years are 'the best of your life', so why had it all seemed so underwhelming? And what did that mean for my future? If that was the high point, what was to follow?

My grandad had died during the third year of my studies and, after graduating, I used the money he left me to travel the world. I was fortunate enough to see the Taj Mahal, the Great Wall of China and the Great Barrier Reef, yet I'd hoped to discover *myself*, and instead I returned home even less sure of who I was, or what I wanted.

I applied for countless jobs, without hearing back from the vast majority of employers, before eventually enrolling on a graduate scheme in hotel management. I lasted all of six months before I quit, realising that I didn't enjoy being blackmailed with negative Tripadvisor reviews by tired guests.

I decided that the solution to all my problems would, of course, be to cavalierly fly to Australia to visit a girl I'd met – and fallen hopelessly for – during my travels. I'd grown up watching *Neighbours* every day, and I held a vague notion that life would be happier Down Under. Maybe that was where I was meant to be. The dream didn't last very long. In fact, I hadn't even left the tarmac at Heathrow before the fantasy was smashed into smithereens: shortly before I boarded the flight she messaged to tell me she was seeing someone else.

I can tell you that twenty-fours is a long time to sit on a plane trying to process bad news. And two weeks alone in Melbourne is even longer when you're heartbroken and you're riding around on the Puffing Billy steam train, alongside happy families and loving couples, realising that you blew all your money on this trip and you have nothing to return to.

Growing up I'd been told I could do anything, that I could achieve whatever I wanted, yet here I was failing at everything. Unemployed, unhappy and unsure of my next steps, I moved into the empty holiday caravan in Dorset. I planned to write a novel, or at least that's what I told everyone. In reality, I didn't even have a plot idea.

A few years earlier, after blacking out playing football, I'd been diagnosed with a cardiac arrhythmia. The statistics and stories of sudden arrhythmic death syndrome had made me realise how short life can be. As life-affirming as having a curative operation was, it also exacerbated my fear that I needed to make the most of my time on the planet. However, as I scrolled through Instagram to see the burgeoning success my friends were enjoying, I was sat alone watching daytime TV. Notably, Ramsay Street no longer looked as shiny.

Even in the Dorset caravan park – virtually empty after the summer's holidaymakers had packed up and gone home – everywhere I looked were reminders of my shortcomings. I turned on the football, and far from being boyhood heroes, the players were now the same age or younger than me. I listened, on repeat, to the one record left in the caravan: Van Morrison's *Moondance*. One of my all-time favourites. Until I realised that Van Morrison was only twenty-four years old when he released it . . . and this was his third album.

What did I have to show for my twenty-four years on the planet? I hadn't played in the Premier League or written one of the greatest albums of all time. In fact, far from crafting my own novel, the only writing I was doing was sending ever-despairing messages to my Australian crush, who by this point had, quite rightly, blocked me on every form of social media. As the Van Morrison record continued to spin, and I stared out at the crashing waves beating against the Jurassic Coast, I wondered what I was going to do.

Where was I going to find happiness, or purpose, or meaning? What was the point to all of this?

I was questioning everything.

And like any millennial, I turned to Google for the answers.

If you ask Google 'What is the meaning of life?', you are greeted with approximately 9,790,000,000 results.

And so, in-between my hectic daily schedule of watching *This Morning* and *Loose Women*, I trawled through essays, newspaper articles, countless YouTube videos, various dictionary definitions and numerous references to the number 42, before I discovered an intriguing project carried out during the 1930s.

Will Durant (1885–1981) was a prolific writer, historian and philosopher, noteworthy for his 1926 book *The Story of Philosophy*, in which he profiled several prominent Western philosophers and their ideas. Shortly after the book's publication, the US was struck by the Great Depression and soon Durant began to receive correspondence asking him about life's meaning. This escalated in 1930 when he was approached by a stranger who told Durant that he was planning on killing himself unless the philosopher could give him a reason not to. Durant offered many reasons, but the stranger seemed unmoved and left. Durant never found out what happened to the man, and the encounter haunted him.

The following year he decided to write to one hundred luminaries across the arts, politics, sciences and religion, asking them about life's meaning and also to relate how they each found meaning, purpose and fulfilment in their own lives. He instructed each to 'write briefly if you must, write at length and at leisure if you possibly can . . .'

While a considerable number asked to be excused, responses came back from Ivy League presidents, Nobel Prize winners, psychologists, novelists, professors, poets, scientists, artists and athletes. His findings were collated in the book *On the Meaning of Life*, published in 1932.

As I hastily downloaded the Kindle version and flicked through the letters – from famous thinkers like Gandhi, Bertrand Russell and Sinclair Lewis – I was intrigued by each of their responses.

And then the idea came to me.

Whether it was simply a way to procrastinate from writing my own novel – for which I was still to think up a plot – or because I had far too much time on my hands, I decided that I should recreate Durant's experiment and seek my own answers.

Surely someone would have the answer to help me.

I decided immediately that I was going to handwrite each letter. I thought that the personal touch would help the letters stand out, and the fact that I didn't have a printer in the caravan clarified my choice. However, I couldn't simply write letters to the great and the good on just any paper. And certainly not using the old, faded scrap paper that sat in the caravan, which was indented with historic Scrabble score tallies.

I opened my laptop to peruse the Paperchase website, and before I knew it I'd added reams of 90gsm parchment paper, complete with matching envelopes, to my online basket. I was stunned when I saw the total price wasn't far short of the cost of my flight back from Melbourne. With precious few funds left in my bank account, I had to sign up to their membership scheme and pretend it was my birthday solely to gain a discount.

I'd also decided that it would be polite to include stamped self-addressed envelopes for the replies, which meant I not only needed double the number of envelopes, but also twice the quantity of stamps. I must admit I hadn't realised quite how much stamps cost. And certainly not how much it costs to send letters abroad. I even had to bid on dozens of American stamps from eBay so I could stick them onto the return envelopes being sent to the States. Before I knew it, the compact caravan had turned into a Royal Mail sorting office.

Undoubtedly, the definition of a 'luminary' has altered enormously from 1931, when Durant's list was mostly full of academics and educators. I wanted my list to be as broad as possible, and I was keen to ensure more diversity considering that, of all the responses published in Durant's book, only three were from women. While it would be impossible to encompass all walks of life, I attempted to contact a cross-section of people, from different backgrounds, countries, gender, sexuality, races and religions – aware, of course, that the final results would be reliant on those who replied.

The list was also highly dependent on who I could find a postal address for. I scoured websites searching for contact details, and spent hours carefully writing the letters, neatly folding them, and sealing them inside the envelopes. I lugged the ones needing a foreign stamp to the post office in the nearest town centre, a thirty-minute walk away, and tried not to look too embarrassed as the gentleman behind the counter curiously browsed the addresses, no doubt wondering why I was writing to US presidents. I licked the stamps, dropped all of the letters into the postbox, and then I waited . . .

We can now communicate instantaneously with people from across the world, via phone, message or even video-call, yet there is still something peculiarly exciting – magical, even – about receiving a letter in the post. When my sister and I were younger, we'd have a competition every school summer holiday to see who could get the most celebrity autographs sent to us. I'd write to footballers and she'd write to the cast of *Only Fools and Horses* (somewhat bizarrely, she was an eleven year old obsessed with the 1980s sitcom). By the end of the summer I'd have a ring-binder full of (often pre-printed) signatures. I still remember the excitement at the sound of the letterbox clattering, as we'd rush from the back garden, race through the hall, barging each other out of the way, to be the first to get our hands on the letters. The postman had been elevated to Father Christmas-like status. I experienced the same palpable excitement as I sat waiting for the responses to my letters now, but this time the postman wasn't as forthcoming. The letterbox didn't clatter. Days, and then weeks, passed with no responses. Nothing. Absolutely nothing.

I began to worry that I'd blown the little money I had on stamps and stationery. What was I thinking? I'd spent hours searching for addresses, handwriting letters and trekking across fields to post them. What if nobody responded? My mind started to flash through all the scenarios. Were the addresses correct? What if they'd all been lost? Had I been stupid posting them all together? Maybe the postbox wasn't functioning any more? Surely at least one person would respond eventually?

And, eventually, they did. Finally a single letter, enclosed in my self-addressed envelope, arrived. This was it. The glorious moment I'd been waiting for. I looked down at my own handwriting, wondering who it was from. What wise words did they have for me? Eager and ecstatic, I tore open the luxurious envelope, and frantically read the contents of the typed letter. The word 'unfortunately' jumped out as if it was written in a font ten times larger than the other words.

It was a rejection. I'd had enough of them already this year.

My heart continued to sink as I received a spate of letters *returned to sender – address unknown*. I started to calculate how much each letter cost me in time and money, just to receive the letter back unopened. Without any explanation, a few signed photographs tumbled through the letterbox. It wasn't what I'd asked for, but at least I thought I could flog them and recoup the postage costs, if nothing else.

It took another couple of weeks until I received the first positive response, if 'positive' is the correct term.

Professor Lord Robert Winston – esteemed scientist and IVF pioneer – had been one of the first names on my list. Who better to ask about life's meaning than the man who has spent his career helping bring life into the world?

I knew all the waiting had been worthwhile as soon as I saw his name on the headed paper.

I read and reread his paragraph, skipping to the stand-out remarks.

'I really do not understand what you mean by the "meaning of life" . . . To my mind, life is a four-letter word . . . I don't think that there is such a meaning . . . I have no idea whether that is the meaning of life.'

Now, picture me sitting alone in this empty caravan, experiencing an existential crisis. I can't exactly say it was the reassuring, life-affirming answer I had naively hoped to receive. I had been looking for a reason for my existence, something to explain where and how I should find purpose and happiness, and now I was being told by one of the country's leading scientists that he hasn't got a clue why we're here either. If he didn't have an answer, then how was I meant to know?

After this, rather excitingly, letters started to drop through my letterbox more regularly.

Professor Lord Winston wasn't the only one to express this sentiment, but others gave a variety of responses, whether they found their meaning in religion, spirituality or in family and friends. Many of the replies surprised me, especially from those who had experienced trauma in their lives and had learned to appreciate life more than those of us who can sometimes take it for granted.

Just as Durant had done, I was also keen to write to someone who had spent their life behind bars, and so I was most intrigued to hear back from the notorious prisoner Charles Salvador aka Charles Bronson, who declared that despite spending four and a half decades in prison he'd found himself and enjoyed his life. If he could 'find himself' in prison, I could surely 'find myself' in a caravan.

During the three months I spent living in the holiday park, walking the cliffs and trying to figure out my life, the responses greatly inspired me. Maybe as Dame Hilary Mantel alluded to in her answer, meaning had emerged for me through the practice of the quest. While I wasn't sure of my own answer, I felt rejuvenated and motivated. I thought back to my global travels and, having been on walking tours in every city I'd visited, I was inspired to set up my own walking tour company in my home city of Bristol, meeting new people every day. I also finally – albeit slowly – got on with writing the novel that I'd told everyone I was going to write. And the heartbreak and worried feelings began to disappear.

For the next few years, I kept the project going on the back-burner, sending out letters when I encountered someone interesting or discovered their story. During this time, though, searching for life's meaning seemed to fade from my priorities; I was too busy to contemplate philosophical matters. Then suddenly the world paused, and we all had time to stop and think. It was during Covid-19 that I dug out the folder full of correspondence. As I reread the responses – still awed that people had taken the time to reply to my odd little letter – I realised how many conversations I'd had in the intervening years with friends who had felt the same way as I had done: lost and confused, trying to find their place and direction in the world. I realised that what started as a personal project could have wider interest. I decided that these letters, which had been gathering dust under my bed, deserved to be shared. I vowed to finish the project that I started.

As I write this introduction, it's nearly nine years since I posted the first letter, and I'm currently sat in the same caravan where the project started. Albeit, this time I'm just here for a week's holiday with my girlfriend. A lot has happened in the intervening time. I'm now older than virtually the entire England football team. *Neighbours* was cancelled and, thankfully, resurrected. I've travelled widely, and lived – at least temporarily – in Paris, New York, Vienna and Florence, but I've never been back to Australia. I've learned how to make choux buns, gnocchi and schnitzel, but I've forgotten absolutely everything I studied at university. I wrote that novel – its plot about a man suffering a quarter-life crisis – and remarkably it was published in over a dozen languages. I've fallen in love. I've seen Van Morrison perform live, twice. And I spent seven years maintaining the lie that my birthday was in September to the shop assistants in Paperchase, until the business went into administration and I felt enormous guilt that my deception had somehow single-handedly caused their downfall.

In those years, less has changed inside the caravan – there's still the battered Rummikub box, the clock which runs slow, the chipped china. Unfortunately, though, underneath the rust has grown, and by the time this book is in the shops, the caravan will have been removed from the site. For perhaps one last time here, I play the Van Morrison record: its tracks 'Caravan', 'Brand New Day' and 'Everyone' a soundtrack to this epoch, and I allow myself a moment to look back.

My worries, my heartbreak, my fear of failure now seem wildly melodramatic – especially in comparison to what some of my incredible contributors have experienced. I cringe at some of my actions, and I laugh at my naivety. I pause to think about my grandad, and my first real experience of death and grief. I feel sad that while I've been able to question so many incredible people, I can't ask Pap for his thoughts, or ask him any more questions about his own life – about the photos we found after his death of him standing by the Pyramids when he served in Egypt. Something he never mentioned once.

But curiously, I remember those strange few months in the caravan not as traumatic, but as nostalgic and life-changing. The hurt, the sense of loss and the soul-searching – all a necessary form of growth, a part of puberty – have been replaced in my memory as a time when I enjoyed the small things, the peace and quiet, the countryside walks, the music, the letter-writing.

After all this time, I'm not sure I still have my own definitive answer, and maybe I never will. Perhaps, as others suggest on the following pages, it's an answer which changes with age.

But I've realised it's good to do crazy things, even if they don't work out how you thought they would. Life is funny like that. So get on that plane and fly across the world to see someone. Move into a caravan. Or write to your musical hero Yusuf/Cat Stevens and ask him what the meaning of life is, for this project certainly brought me meaning, purpose and happiness.

I sincerely hope you can take something from these letters just as I did. What follows are the responses presented in their original form. From philosophers to politicians, pop-stars to playwrights and presidents to prisoners. Some were handwritten, some were typed, some were emailed. Some were scrawled on pieces of scrap paper. Some on parchment. Some are pithy one-liners. Some are lengthy memoirs. Some are poignant. Some simply amusing.

And once you've finished reading this book, please do send me your own thoughts and stories. I'd love to hear your opinion.

Write briefly if you must; write at length and at leisure if you possibly can . . .

James Bailey, April 2024
www.JamesBaileyWrites.com

The Letter

In 1931, philosopher Will Durant wrote to 100 luminaries in the arts, politics, religion and sciences, challenging them to respond not only to the fundamental question of life's meaning but also to relate how they each found meaning, purpose and fulfilment in their own lives.

I am currently replicating Durant's study, and I'd be most appreciative if you could tell me what you think the meaning of life is, and how you find meaning, purpose and fulfilment in your own life?

As Durant originally instructed, 'Write briefly if you must; write at length and at leisure if you possibly can.'

Thank you very much for your time.

Yours sincerely,
James Bailey

DAME JANE GOODALL

HELEN SHARMAN OBE

BINDI IRWIN

DR ASTRO TELLER

CATHERINE COLEMAN FLOWERS

LIZZIE CARR MBE

PROFESSOR JEAN GOLDING OBE

PROFESSOR IAN FRAZER AC

DR MICHAEL IRWIN

PROFESSOR ANIL SETH

SIR TIM SMIT KBE

EDWARD O. WILSON

DR MYA-ROSE CRAIG

PROFESSOR LORD ROBERT WINSTON

BILL McKIBBEN

HENRY MARSH CBE FRCS

DR KATHRYN MANNIX

Scientists & Environmentalists

Dame
JANE GOODALL

DAME JANE GOODALL is a conservationist, anthropologist, the world's foremost expert on chimpanzees and a UN Messenger of Peace. Since she first visited Gombe Stream National Park, Tanzania, in 1960, she has spent over sixty years studying the social and family interactions of wild chimpanzees. In 1977, Goodall established the Jane Goodall Institute (JGI), to support the Gombe research and scale up the protection of chimpanzees in their habitats. In 2018 she was nominated as one of the greatest figures of the twentieth century on the BBC show *Icons*. In 2022, Mattel Inc. unveiled a new Barbie doll in her likeness, which the toymaker says is made from recycled plastic, as part of its Inspiring Women Series.

The Jane Goodall Institute

16.1.18

Dear James,

Sorry it took me a while
to get your letter as I am
not often home - but was
for Christmas - then got flu.
I will try & find time to
answer your question - but when
is your deadline?

Best communicate by
e mail.

Warm regards,
Jane Goodall.

WHAT IS THE MEANING OF LIFE? Only the Creator can answer. What is the meaning of my life? Perhaps that is for others to judge, when I am no longer living it, when they can see how my little moment of eternity had meaning in the whole big picture – if indeed it did. But when it comes to how I find meaning, purpose and fulfilment in my own life that is something I can answer.

My maternal grandfather was a Congregational minister – sadly he died before I was born, but I heard a great deal about him. I was five years old when World War II broke out. My father joined the army. His brother, in the air force, was shot down and killed. My mother took me and my sister to live in Bournemouth, England, with her mother, two unmarried sisters – and her brother, a surgeon who diverted all his energy to those wounded in the blitz of London, came home exhausted every other weekend. (That same house is home today, shared with my sister and her family.) I constantly heard of friends and relatives being killed and the horror of war gradually grew. But the real nightmare for me came with the release of photos of the victims of the Holocaust. For the first time I wrestled with the existence of evil. How could a loving God allow such horrors as war, torture and mass killing to happen? Did God exist? I continued thinking about this, and when I was about fourteen years old I had come to the conclusion that, perhaps, life on earth, starting with a single celled organism and culminating with the complex plants and animals we know today, is simply an experiment. If so humans, I thought, were a mistake, along with leeches, mosquitoes, tsetse flies and the like. We had huge potential – I thought of the saints, the great architecture and literature, art and music, medicine, technology and so on. But we were so destructive.

Today when we look at the impact of humans on the planet we are appalled at how we are harming the environment: think of overpopulation, abject poverty, unsustainable lifestyles, loss of biodiversity and now climate change.

The behaviour study of Gombe National Park chimpanzees that I began in 1960 shows that they are more like us than any other living creature. There are striking similarities between them and us in the structure of our DNA, immune system, blood and anatomy of the brain. And, as well, chimpanzees are highly intelligent, use and make tools, show

'Everywhere I go there are young people with shining eyes wanting to tell me what they have been doing to make this a better world.'

similarities in the postures and gestures of non-verbal communication, and have a long childhood during which the cultural behaviours of their community are passed from one generation to the next, emphasising the importance of learning by observation. Chimpanzees wage a sort of primitive warfare and can be brutally aggressive. Like us they may kill each other. And like us they show love, compassion, true altruism, and experience emotions, similar to or the same as ours, such as happiness, sadness, anger, depression and grief. And they have a sense of humour. (We now know that many other animals also show highly developed social and intellectual behaviour.) But only we humans have developed the power of spoken language. So we can teach about things not present, plan for the distant future, discuss ideas and articulate abstract ideals. It is this, I believe, that has played a major role in the explosive development of our intellect.

I discovered in 1984 that chimpanzees were decreasing in number across their range in Africa as forests were destroyed, as the bushmeat trade grew (the commercial hunting of wild animals for food), as mothers were shot to capture their infants for sale as pets, for zoos, circuses and medical research, and as humans penetrated deeper into the forests thus exposing chimpanzees to human diseases, all of which they can catch. After learning this I knew I had to try to do something to help them and that I must leave the forest that I loved.

(1) I visited several range countries to see the situation regarding the chimpanzees for myself – something I think is important. I saw the effect of logging, I saw chimpanzee infants for sale in the markets, kept as pets only to be shut in tiny cages or attached to chains when they got older, unmanageable, potentially dangerous. I saw them in terrible zoos. The Jane Goodall Institute (JGI) was able to create sanctuaries where these orphans could be cared for. (2) At the same time I learned about the plight of so many people living in and around chimpanzee habitat – the desperate poverty, lack of education and health facilities and growing populations –

and I knew I had to try to do something to help *them*. And (3) I managed to visit some medical research facilities using chimpanzees – in the USA, Austria and the Netherlands (some of the worst experiences in my life to see our closest relatives in 5' X 5' X 7' high cages surrounded by metal bars, undergoing painful experiments). (4) I also visited a number of zoos in the US and Europe, noting the often cramped quarters, inappropriate groupings and lack of enrichment (to counteract boredom). Once I knew about these four dire situations I metaphorically rolled up my sleeves and planned what could be done.

When I began my research in Gombe in 1960 the national park was part of the great forest belt stretching across Africa. When I flew over the area in the mid-1980s I was shocked to see the national park was a little island of forest surrounded by bare hills. More people living there than the land could support, too poor to buy food elsewhere, struggling to survive. They were cutting down trees to make land for growing more food or to make money from charcoal or timber. That's when it hit me that unless we could find ways for these people to make a living without destroying their environment we couldn't save chimps, forests, or anything else. So in 1994 JGI initiated Tacare, a very holistic programme that included restoring fertility to over-used farmland (without chemicals!), water management, scholarships to give girls a chance for secondary education, microfinance opportunities and family planning information. Villagers learned to monitor the health of their village forest reserves using smart phones. Gradually they came to understand that protecting the environment was not just for wildlife but for their own future. They became our partners in conservation. That programme has been truly successful: what started in the twelve villages around Gombe is now in 104 villages through most of the chimps' range in Tanzania, and also operates in six other African countries where we work with chimpanzees. If you fly over Gombe today there are no more bare hills – the trees are growing back along with biodiversity.

JGI has the largest sanctuary for chimpanzees orphaned by the bushmeat trade and ex pets in Africa, in the Republic of Congo and a smaller one in South Africa. We actually started two more, in Uganda and Kenya, but they are now operated by others, which is lucky as they are very costly to maintain.

I began working to improve the conditions of captive chimps with a programme called ChimpanZoo, which emphasized the importance of alleviating boredom by introducing all sorts of enrichment activities – including artificial termite mounds with narrow tunnels through which the chimpanzees pushed straws to fish for mustard, which they love. It also gave students a chance to observe and record chimpanzee behaviour. Enrichment activities were also introduced into the terrible medical research labs, which helped a little during the many years when JGI and other organizations worked to bring this research to an end. In fact this did not happen in America until it was found that none of the experiments being done in America eight years ago were either beneficial or even potentially beneficial to human health. All but a very few, believed to be too old to move, are now living out their lives in sanctuaries. Chimpanzees had already moved to sanctuaries in the Netherlands and Austria where I had also visited two large laboratories.

After getting my Ph.D. (in animal behaviour) I began travelling around the world raising awareness about the true nature of animals and the importance of conserving the natural world. And on all continents I met – and still meet – people, including young people, who seemed to have lost all hope. They understand the problems but feel helpless and do nothing. I met high school and university students who were depressed, angry, mostly apathetic. Why? 'Because,' they told me, 'our future has been compromised and there is nothing we can do about it.' We have compromised their future – but there IS something they – all of us – can do about it. In 1991, I started Roots & Shoots, a programme to give young people hope through action. Each group chooses three projects: to help people, to help animals, to help the environment. Then they roll up their sleeves and take action. Today there are thousands of groups in seventy countries, with members from kindergarten through university and more and more adults taking part.

The most important message of R&S – and for *all* of us – is that each one of us matters and has a role to play, each one of us makes some impact on the planet – every day. Think about the cumulative effect if millions, billions of people thought about the consequence of their choices as to what they bought. Did its production harm the environment? Did it involve cruelty to animals as in the unspeakably cruel factory farms? Is it cheap because of unfair wages or slave labour? If so, don't buy it. And this can lead to consumer pressure and create change in business practices.

Let me return to the questions I was asked. I found meaning in my life by living among and writing and talking about chimpanzees, and purpose when I went on the road to try to persuade people to help make this a better world for animals and people. It is very meaningful to me when people tell me they now understand why it is wrong to use chimpanzees or elephants in a circus, why they should avoid factory farmed meat, food that has been industrially produced (especially GM foods), and all the rest. It is meaningful when people who joined R&S as children tell me how it changed their attitude towards animals, the environment – and the future. When people in China tell me that of course they care about the environment and animals – they were in the R&S movement in primary school. And when everywhere I go there are young people with shining eyes wanting to tell me what they have been doing to make this a better world. And the many adults who tell me, after my lectures or after reading some of my books, that they now have some hope for the future, and will do their bit.

Now that I have written the above about my life, it seems that it must have been meaningful not only for me, but for hundreds of chimpanzees and other animals whose lives have been improved. For countless Africans who have begun to rise out of poverty through involvement with our JGI programmes. And for hundreds and thousands who are taking or have taken part in R&S activities And this, of course, means that my life does seem to have been worth while.

I probably have a number of years left. I have been granted very good health – that stood me in good stead now that I have turned ninety. I want to give hope to hundreds of thousands more young people. There are so many animal welfare nightmares that I want to try to mitigate. There are so many 'developments' – such as dams – and commercial activities – such as fracking – that should be halted, as they are harming the environment and wildlife. There are so many animals and plants so highly endangered by human activity that they are on the verge of extinction – indeed, we are in the midst of the 6th great extinction. There are thousands of communities, and many countries, where I still would love to visit and spread some of the understanding. Above all I want to give hope to those who have lost or are losing hope. For if we lose hope we become apathetic or fall into deep despair, and do nothing. If we look at the state of the world, with terrible wars in Ukraine and Gaza, fifteen wars across Africa, with uprisings in other parts of the world, with poverty on the one hand and greedy unsustainable lifestyles on the other, with refugees and migrants, and with climate change and resultant terrifying storms, floods, droughts, heatwaves and wild fires – well, it is not surprising that people are losing hope. So I must share my stories, share why I still have hope. First, the energy, commitment and enthusiasm of young people once they know the problems and are empowered to take action – they are truly changing the world. Then there is the human intellect – science is coming up with innovative technology such as renewable energy to enable us to live in better harmony with nature and we are beginning to think about our own carbon footprints as we go through each day. Then nature is amazingly resilient and will return to places we have utterly destroyed given time and sometimes some help, and animals on the brink of extinction can be given another chance. And finally the indomitable spirit that enables some people to tackle what seems impossible and succeed.

I was born with all sorts of gifts, but very important is the gift of communication, writing and speaking. So that people listen to my stories and are inspired to make a difference. And this does indeed give purpose to my life.

One last pondering. We cannot choose our parents – but I was lucky in that I had the very best of mothers. When everyone laughed at my ten-year-old dream of going to Africa she simply told me I would have to work hard, take advantage of opportunities, and not to give up. Could that have been part of some overall plan to give that young girl a good start in life? Sometimes I feel that things which seemed like coincidences were, in fact, opportunities that I was free to seize – or ignore. The dog Rusty who taught me so much was not even ours. He lived in a hotel round the corner, came to us at six a.m. and barked to come in. He went home for lunch, then spent the rest of the day and evening with me until bedtime (the owners knew and were fine with it). When all my friends were moved to a higher class, I was left down, depressed and chagrined – and thus was in the class of the friend who would invite me to Africa so that I would meet Louis Leakey and have the chance to study not just any animal, but the one most like us. And so many little things since – I met the man who would become chair of JGI-UK when we sat next to each other on a plane that neither of us was meant to be on. And he was a very prestigious lawyer and offered me protection when I stood up to the powerful pharmaceutical company that was using chimpanzees in horrible conditions, and which had issued seventy-two law suits against anyone who criticised them. And I could go on and on. Coincidences? Or part of a plan?

To sum up: 'The fault,' says the Bard, 'lies not in our stars but in ourselves that we are underlings.' But the stars have certainly played a part in my life.

HELEN
SHARMAN OBE

HELEN SHARMAN became the first British astronaut to visit the Mir Space Station in May 1991. After responding to a radio advertisement asking for applicants to be the first British space explorer, Sharman was selected for the mission, ahead of nearly 13,000 other applicants, and underwent eighteen months of intensive training. Sharman spent eight days orbiting the Earth, and conducted a variety of experiments, including measurements of the Earth's atmosphere, medical and agricultural tasks. After returning from space, Sharman has spent many years communicating science and its benefits.

I INTERPRET 'LIFE'S MEANING' in two ways.

The first and most obvious (to me) expansion of the phrase 'life's meaning' is 'the meaning of life'. At the risk of annoying philosophers, I can explain my thoughts very simply because in my view there is no meaning of life. We are temporary accumulations of various arrangements of the chemical elements of which we are composed, the ordered outcome of a series of reactions of an increasingly complex web of interactions. We can debate what is life itself (animals, plants, bacteria, viruses, ecosystems, the Earth, even – it depends on what the definer of the term wants to include) but as far as I can see, there is no intended purpose of life in general; life just happens.

I am sure that some lives are brought into being in order to fulfil certain roles: an heir, a carer for the family, an organ donor for a sick relative, perhaps to do something that a parent always wanted to do themselves. This might be the purpose for which they were conceived, but it is not the meaning of their lives. (It may or may not become meaning in their lives, which I argue is different.)

So to my other interpretation of 'life's meaning', which is 'the meaning in life'. This must be different for different people, so I will answer only for myself here.

Having a sense of purpose is important to us all and helps us to have 'meaning'. I have had various ambitions over the course of my life so far that have led me to carry out a range of activities. My time in space, though, kick-started one purpose in particular that has been with me ever since, and this is to have more people considering science to be part of life. In the same way that music, art and language are not separated from who we are, science should not be regarded as something to be studied or researched in isolation. I want loads more of us to participate in social debate about how best the world should use science, questioning the headlines and leaders' ideas in a logical, non-reactionary manner. This can influence decision makers, especially in democracies, and ultimately makes the world a better place.

When I hear of any positive impact I have made by communicating science and its benefits towards this purpose, I get a partial sense of fulfilment. I say partial, because this particular purpose is unlikely ever to be completed. (However much people are attuned to science and logic, no democracy is perfect.)

Fulfilment from the impact of actions that are carried out with a purpose in mind is my best attempt at a simple definition of 'meaning'. However, I would say that there is also meaning in the learning or self-improvement that is necessary to understand the world and oneself, in order better to fulfil a purpose.

But the biggest sense of fulfilment I have comes from living life in a different way since my spaceflight. Not long after I returned to Earth, I realised that what I had not thought about once in space was the material items that I own or aspire to own. On board the Space Station, I had the basics of what I needed to survive relatively comfortably, e.g. shelter, food and water, even some company. But what astronauts miss most, particularly the astronauts who have been away from Earth for more than a few weeks, is the rich variety of human relationships and being in close contact, physically and mentally, with the individuals we know and love. When we looked out of the window, we liked to spot places we recognised and where our loved ones were. We would talk about our families, friends and work colleagues when we flew over the places they lived.

That day back on Earth, thinking about my time in space, I realised that I needed to change my priorities. There is nothing wrong with wanting to improve our quality of life and we all need a certain amount of material items to live comfortably, but being in space taught me that over and above material stuff, what is really important is the relationships – the people (and animals) – in our lives. And I am a different person because of that. I am freed from the purpose to buy stuff in order to be thought of in a certain way, to 'keep up' with others. Instead, I can focus on what really matters, and that puts meaning into my life.

Either way I look at it, whether it's encouraging society to embrace science or de-emphasising material items in favour of relationships, people are at the centre of meaning in my life.

Helen Sharman, October 2023

BINDI IRWIN

BINDI IRWIN is a conservationist who inherited her love of wildlife from her parents: the late conservationist and television personality Steve Irwin, and Terri Irwin, the current owner of Australia Zoo. Irwin made her television debut through *The Crocodile Hunter* and, aged nine, hosted *Bindi the Jungle Girl*, a children's wildlife documentary TV series. She won Season 21 of *Dancing with the Stars* (US), and currently stars alongside her mother Terri and her younger brother Robert in *Crikey! It's the Irwins*.

What is the meaning of life?
This is the question that has haunted
almost every dreamer, believer and out of
the box thinker for time immemorial.
This is the very question that drives me
forward each and every day. Because,
like many things in life, I don't think
that there is one clear answer.
However, since I was a little girl my
mum always taught me that there is
one very special ingredient to life, which
she believed, will forever be the purpose
for each and every one of us.
Unconditional love.

Out of every possible answer to the
meaning of life, Mum's is my favourite.
Unconditional love, something so pure
and good, a feeling we can have for a
million different things, people, animals, places.

Which leads me to the next part of my question. What is our purpose in life? That is not so clearly answered either. You have to follow your own path to be able to find what you truly love in life. What brings the most light to your heart. You may have to try a hundred things that don't stick to find what you are truly passionate about. Or perhaps something or someone has stuck with you so fiercely that you have already found your own unconditional love and purpose. If the latter is true, consider yourself one of the lucky ones. Because most of us are born with the question of the meaning and purpose of life buried deep down in our souls, and finding the answer, or what you feel to be the answer, can be quite the journey. I personally believe that we all live several lives in one lifetime. Each new chapter is an opportunity to leave your own legacy and try to answer the questions of what is the meaning and purpose of your own life.

I hope to use my time and energy to help protect wildlife and wild places. My home at Australia Zoo, the wildlife we save through our charity, Wildlife Warriors, that is my purpose. And the love in my heart for my family, that feels like my meaning.

And maybe that unconditional love that fills our souls really is the meaning of it all. ♡ I'd like to think so.

WHAT IS THE MEANING OF LIFE? This is the question that has haunted almost every dreamer, believer and out of the box thinker for time immemorial. This is the very question that drives me forward each and every day. Because, like many things in life, I don't think that there is one clear answer. However, since I was a little girl my mum always taught me that there is one very special ingredient to life, which she believed, will forever be the purpose for each and every one of us.

Unconditional love.

Out of every possible answer to the meaning of life, Mum's is my favourite. Unconditional love, something so pure and good, a feeling we can have for a million different things, animals, places.

Which leads me to the next part of my question. What is our purpose in life? That is not so clearly answered either. You have to follow your own path to be able to find what you truly love in life. What brings the most light to your heart. You may have to try a hundred things that don't stick to find what you are truly passionate about. Or perhaps something or someone has stuck with you so fiercely that you have already found your own unconditional love and purpose. If the latter is true, consider yourself one of the lucky ones. Because most of us are born with the question of the meaning and purpose of life buried deep down in our souls, and finding the answer, or what you feel to be the answer, can be quite the journey. I personally believe that we all live several lives in one lifetime. Each new chapter is an opportunity to leave your own legacy and try to answer the questions of what is the meaning and purpose of your own life.

I hope to use my time and energy to help protect wildlife and wild places. My home at Australia Zoo, the wildlife we save through our charity, Wildlife Warriors, that is my purpose. And the love in my heart for my family, that feels like my meaning.

And maybe that unconditional love that fills our souls really is the meaning of it all. I'd like to think so.

'My mum always taught me that there is one very special ingredient to life … Unconditional love.'

Dr ASTRO TELLER

DR ASTRO TELLER is the co-founder and Captain of Moonshots (CEO) of X, which is Alphabet's moonshot factory for inventing and launching breakthrough technologies designed to help tackle huge problems in the world. Notable projects include Google Glass, Google Brain and Waymo (Google Self-Driving Car Project). Prior to X, Teller founded five companies, and taught at Stanford University. He's the successful author of three published books, an international speaker on technology and innovation, and holds a Ph.D. in artificial intelligence from Carnegie Mellon University.

WHEN I RECEIVED YOUR REQUEST, I thought, Sure, I'm happy to write a letter on the meaning of life. I know what I believe – that part is easy. But it's turned out to be a really interesting journey for me to unpack how I got to my beliefs.

When I think back, I remember being on the side of a soccer field when I was ten years old. I was really nervous about the game and how I would perform, but I had this moment of thinking: *Why am I so nervous? There's literally nothing at stake, it's a soccer game, no one's going to die.* And so I had a dual experience standing on the side of the soccer field, of being both really nervous about the outcome and my performance, and simultaneously having a very nihilistic view of *why am I feeling like this when it's all just meaningless.*

Then it clicked that the soccer game doesn't come with inherent meaning. But you can imbue it with meaning. And I wasn't going to have much fun on the field if I didn't commit to some meaning while I was playing. This thought was quickly followed by: *Oh my God, it's not just soccer that you need to imbue with whatever meaning you choose, you need to do that with your life.* If you want to have fun in your life it's critical that you imbue it with meaning and life is no less meaningful for you having imbued it with meaning yourself, rather than it having come from a higher power.

About two years later, I learned to play contract bridge with my grandfathers, Edward Teller and Gerard Debreu. When you play contract bridge, you play with a partner. In duplicate bridge tournaments, the cards are dealt at a circle of tables, you and your partner play the hand against another team at one of the tables, you get as many points as you can, and then the teams who are north–south on the tables move clockwise, and the east–west teams all move counterclockwise. Then the cards are dealt into the identical hands of cards on each table. You move with your partner, you never see the same opposing team twice, and you never see the same hand twice. Lots of teams are playing the identical hands, which allows teams to compare themselves to how other teams did with the same luck that they had.

Duplicate bridge helped me realize that part of the point of life is you can get lucky, but you should not take any pride associated with your privilege or luck. Pride should come in how well you play your cards, your luck in life – all the exogenous factors of your DNA, your family, everything else – relative to how other people would have played those same cards.

A year or two after that, I had an epiphany when I was on a hike in the Tetons. The realization was that we're all novelists writing the story of our life. We are the protagonist in that novel we're writing. We have wildly more control than we pretend to over what that protagonist does, and also who that protagonist becomes. The phrase that really stuck with me was: *be yourself, but on purpose.* On purpose, not in the sense that you're inauthentic or that you wear a mask, but that you can craft who you are and who you will become while being authentic each moment in how you share yourself with the world.

Having gotten to this point where I'm the novelist writing the story of my life, my first temptation was to just go all in on having a positive effect on the world. And that probably came from some implicit, and maybe explicit, pressure from who both of my grandfathers were, because they both had a very large impact on the world. But the more I sat with it, the more that kind of single dimensional meaning to life felt like a crushing pressure.

Where I landed is, if you think of a triangle, at the top of the triangle is essentially all of the ripple effects we leave in the world. Every person you care for, every product or novel or company or painting you create, every person you mentor, every door you hold open for somebody, every person you don't say good morning to, every one of those things is a ripple effect that we leave in the world.

Part of what would make me proud at the end of my protagonist's story – and what would make me feel it had been a life well-lived – is to have left as much of a positive impact on the world as I could manage. I don't just mean the scale of that positive impact. We can't fully control the 'what' of our lives, but we can control our 'how' – we can control how we show up. In all little and big ways, finding ways to leave these really positive ripple effects in the world is what I would call the meaning of life.

But by itself, that triangle would just fall over, it would be top heavy. So I think of one of the corners at the bottom as 'taking care of yourself'. That is the little stuff like flossing every night, brushing your teeth, getting exercise, going to the doctor, investing in yourself, doing things that might not be fun right now, but are going to be good for future-Astro, etc.

And then the other corner is 'having fun'. If you don't find ways to have joy, laughter, silliness, and pleasure in life, you won't have a foundation from which you can actually project a lot of positivity into the world. I'm very lucky that I'm married to someone who I'm completely, madly in love with. We've been married for a long time. And I love my children, I love my many friends, my parents and brother, etc. So, loving and being loved is at the heart of that triangle.

I understand my own beliefs a little better now for having had to explain them in this letter. Isn't it wonderful the way the story of our life unfolds?

CATHERINE
COLEMAN FLOWERS

CATHERINE COLEMAN FLOWERS is an environmental and climate justice activist bringing attention to the largely invisible problem of inadequate waste and water sanitation infrastructure in rural communities in the United States. As the founder of the Center for Rural Enterprise and Environmental Justice (CREEJ), Flowers has spent her career promoting equal access to clean water, air, sanitation and soil to reduce health and economic disparities in marginalised, rural communities. She is the vice chair of the White House Environmental Justice Advisory Council, a MacArthur Fellow for Environmental Health Advocacy, and was recognised as one of *Time*'s '100 Most Influential People' in the world in 2023.

EVERY DAY, WHEN I WAKE UP and see the sun gleaming through my windows, I am thankful for another prospect to grow and learn. Traveling the world and seeing the commonality as well as the differences of each culture I encounter expands my meaning and appreciation of life. Whether it is in Seoul, Tokyo, Honolulu, Lowndes County, Alabama, Detroit or Aspen, my life is enhanced by each new experience. A recent trip to Dubai broadened my horizons as I encountered the sights, sounds and smells of Bedouin culture and innovation. As the desert sun directed its gaze onto my forehead, I was alive with the knowledge that people lived here thousands of years before me. Seeing beautiful buildings like the Museum of the Future that seemingly defy gravity, reminded me of the Pyramids and how long humans have walked the Earth. The welcomes I have received from people around the world reinforce my belief in what a world without arbitrary barriers and peace could be.

Locally, my grandchildren and the students I meet and get to encourage provide an opportunity to continue to make a positive impact for generations to come. Bridging gaps and planting seeds that will germinate and blossom into new thinking, providing sustenance for creativity, sustainability and resilience are all meaningful parts of life. It is that amazing circle that allows me to share stories of my experiences and provide inspiration to the youth that were passed from my ancestors to me. Life is beautiful, and I want to express gratitude to all who I have encountered and have made my journey so meaningful. Thank you.

To me, the meaning of life is to ensure a liveable planet where generations present and future can live in peace. This is what drives my work as an environmental justice activist. I want to be part of leaving the world better than I found it. Contributing to the future prosperity of humanity is what I believe to be the meaning of life.

'To me, the meaning of life is to ensure a liveable planet where generations present and future can live in peace.'

LIZZIE CARR MBE

LIZZIE CARR is the founder of Planet Patrol; a non-profit with the global mission to tackle plastic pollution. In 2016, she became the first person in history to paddle board the length of Britain's waterways, solo and unsupported. In 2017, she was the first woman to paddle board solo across the English Channel, and a year later she became the first person to paddle board the entire length of the Hudson River in America. During these journeys, she photographed and catalogued every single piece of plastic she spotted along the way, subsequently launching Planet Patrol after seeing how flooded our waterways are with plastic pollution. She sparked a worldwide movement that has involved 15,000 people and removed more than 400 tonne bags of rubbish from natural spaces.

OVER THE LAST TEN YEARS, I have come to realise that meaning, purpose and fulfilment are not fixed destinations, instead they are fluid, inherently personal and subject to change as we navigate the unpredictable ebbs and flows of our life experiences. I don't believe we find meaning or purpose, it finds us.

After an unexpected cancer diagnosis in 2013, when I was twenty-six, the question of meaning and purpose – that we can sometimes spend a lifetime trying to answer – became crystal clear.

At the time, cancer felt like my worst nightmare had come true. Now I reflect back on that experience, and the lessons it taught me, as one of my greatest blessings. I barely recognise the person I was before my diagnosis.

Cancer was the catalyst that fundamentally changed my outlook. I no longer found fulfilment in the same ways. It forced me to reevaluate and my earlier life priorities of pay cheques, job titles and getting on the property ladder paled into insignificance. It pushed me out of autopilot and gave me the confidence to explore and pursue a new and unconventional way of living, without apology.

I felt beyond grateful for my second chance, especially when people around me didn't get that opportunity. A combination of trying to make sense of my own existence and survivor's guilt made me adamant to live a life I was in love with, and proud of, every single day.

By chance, I took up paddleboarding shortly after I completed radiotherapy treatment. The water brought me a deep and unexpected sense of connection to nature. There's something very calming and soothing about blue spaces and it became my happy place. Somewhere I could go and rely on to help gather my thoughts, decompress, and figure things out.

But the more time I spent on the water, the more horrified I became by scenes of pollution I witnessed on an almost daily basis. The real turning point was seeing a bird's nest, on Regent's Canal in London, made up almost entirely of plastic bags, wrappers, straws and lids. These precious waterways and the wildlife that relied on them to survive were in a desperate situation and I couldn't turn a blind eye.

The waterways were there for me consistently and without fail when I needed them during recovery, and I wanted to give something back and help restore their health the way they had mine.

In that moment I knew I had found a new sense of purpose. I channelled everything into bettering our waterways. It became all consuming but it never felt like work, because it gave meaning to my time.

In the following three years I went on to complete three world first paddleboarding endurance challenges – all to collect data on water pollution and bring awareness to the issues they [the waterways] face. I wrote a best-selling paddling guidebook about the UK's most beautiful, unrivalled and underestimated waterways, and I set up an environmental non-profit called Planet Patrol.

During my time on the water I have witnessed the spectrum of humanity. I have seen the very best in acts of kindness, selfless volunteering and campaigning and the very worst through mindless littering and the impact of poor water quality.

I do know that it was only until I experienced, first hand, the plight of our waterways that I connected myself personally with the issues they face. I wasn't in search of purpose, it found me because I had fallen in love with our waterways and we protect what we care about.

Now, through my work at Planet Patrol, I dedicate my time to creating paddleboarding and data collection experiences on the water, to help deepen connections with nature and collect valuable data about our precious blue spaces.

When I'm instructing, my advice for standing up successfully on a paddle board is to keep paddling, don't idle and always look in the direction you want to go. It's good advice for life.

'I don't believe we find meaning or purpose, it finds us.'

Professor
JEAN GOLDING OBE

PROFESSOR JEAN GOLDING is an epidemiologist who founded the Avon Longitudinal Study of Parents and Children, known informally as the Children of the Nineties study. It is the most detailed project of its kind anywhere in the world, having followed the lives of children who were born in Avon during 1991 and 1992, and has helped scientists make important discoveries about everything from peanut allergies to the effects of long-Covid. It has collected more than 1.5 million biological samples, including blood, placenta, hair, nails and teeth, along with thousands of questionnaires. Golding was awarded an OBE for services to medical science in 2012, and today is Emeritus Professor of Paediatric and Perinatal Epidemiology at the University of Bristol.

I'VE BEEN ASKED TO DO many difficult things, but this task is one of the more taxing. What do I see as my meaning in life? Having thought about this now, possibly for the first time, I realise that I do recognise a meaning that has been influencing my life for many decades.

In order to understand how that developed over time I have had to go back through my early years. My parents were from slightly different social backgrounds – my father was the son of a Methodist lay preacher; he had had a difficult childhood – his mother had died before his first birthday and his father died when he was aged thirteen. His father had been a successful builder and then became a shopkeeper. However, he had gone bankrupt shortly before he died and my father had to leave school at age fourteen and start work in order to help support his stepmother. At the time he married my mother (shortly before the start of the Second World War) he was still a clerk on a very low wage. During the war, because he was in a listed occupation, he continued with this work but contributed throughout to support the local community in a variety of ways. At the end of the War he was promoted and gradually moved to different parts of Britain with me, my mother and my two younger brothers.

In contrast, my mother's parents were from a more educated class – her father was the son of a Church of England clergyman and her mother the daughter of a scientist. They had emigrated to Canada and that was where my mother was born. I have recently been reading letters my grandmother had written in the 1950s. It was clear that she had been very much involved in that small farming community in the Prairies.

However, it was not my grandparents that had the biggest influence on me during my childhood – they were on the other side of the Atlantic – but rather my great aunts on both sides of the family. The youngest sister of my maternal grandmother was fun and interested in a variety of topics, including detective stories (Agatha Christie in particular); she was looking after her mother in the same Cornish town, but was an artist, always bright and cheerful and a joy to know. The other great aunts were sisters of my maternal grandfather. As daughters of a clergyman they were devout, but also had taken up a variety of professions and interests. One had learned to carve and had taught men in her village to do so – together they had carved the ends of the pews in their local church; another had become an Anglican nun and spent most of her life teaching children in India; another had become a physiotherapist and a PE school teacher.

That was the background. My personal history also had a part to play. In my pre-school years I had had a complex medical history resulting in prolonged hospital stays. At this time in the UK the policy was that parents should only be allowed to visit their hospitalised children for short periods of time – in my case it was just for once a week. I don't remember the details but it was clearly traumatic – for twenty years afterwards the smell of the disinfectant used and the type of food I had been given in hospital would bring me out in a cold sweat. My mother says that when I was finally discharged I was very clingy and anxious. Although I thereafter found it difficult to interact with others, I enjoyed school and thrived on learning.

Fast forward to my teenage years. The family had moved to the north of England, where my father's job had taken him. I had started a new school which I found very different from what I was used to – and within two weeks I had caught polio. This resulted in my suddenly losing the ability to use my arms and legs. I was transported to a hospital where I was isolated for a few weeks. After that it was an extensive period of exercising so that gradually some of my muscles started working again, although those in my left leg remained very feeble. The timing of this was difficult as I had no local social support. I had not attended school long enough to have made any friends, and I was embarrassed by the fact that my contemporaries felt sorry for me.

Nowadays I remember very little about that period of my life – but everything changed when I got to University. This was turning a page and starting new friendships and interests. I loved it.

Among the many contacts I made, I fell for a man who I subsequently married. This turned out not to be a brilliant move. At the point at which it became likely that my children would suffer I became more self-confident and managed to persuade him to leave. Subsequently I divorced him. Thereafter I was a single mother bringing up two small children.

I think this was the point at which my meaning of life was crystallising. By that time I had a supportive and interesting social network in London and had started working in the field of epidemiology. It was absolutely clear that two things were most important – one was to bring up my children to the best of my ability, and the other was epidemiology. This field studies disorder and development and tries to determine ways in which these are influenced by features of the environment. It needs an enquiring mind and is basically a detective story. One discovers the facts and then tries to make coherent sense of them to understand how and why one type of environment might prompt a disorder to occur, to be followed ideally by developing possible preventive strategies.

One feature of my life that was formative, and of which I have never spoken before, was what I can only describe as profound and unexpected spiritual experiences. The first of these occurred when I had polio and was in isolation, and the second was on the morning of the day in which I was to give evidence at my divorce hearing. In both instances there was a strong feeling of warmth that suffused and supported me. The results have been quite life changing. I was able to cope with polio and disability without feeling any resentment or bitterness, and I was able to accept the divorce as a positive achievement rather than a failure (which I had felt up until then).

I have read elsewhere that people who have had out-of-body experiences are never afraid of death. I certainly have not been afraid of death but am always aware that there is so much more that I want to complete before that happens.

I have followed many of the Christian teachings. Although I have doubts about the factual accuracy of details of much of the Christian story I have always felt that it really didn't matter whether the details were true or not – the message is told in allegories which often contain meaningful messages. One parable which had a major influence on me was the parable of the talents – although apparently about investing money profitably, it can be interpreted as investing in one's physical or mental talents. This is something that I frequently remind myself of – my talent is in studying people and the way in which the environments in which they live affects their health and wellbeing. This is where I find my fulfilment, as well as in my interactions with family and friends.

Jean Golding, January 2024

'I certainly have not been afraid of death but am always aware that there is so much more that I want to complete before that happens.'

Professor
IAN FRAZER AC

PROFESSOR IAN FRAZER is the co-inventor of the technology enabling the HPV vaccines, currently used worldwide to help prevent cervical cancer. He works as a clinician scientist, having trained as a clinical immunologist. As a professor at the University of Queensland, he leads a research group working on the immunobiology of epithelial cancers, and he heads a biotechnology company working on new vaccine technologies. He chairs the Australian Medical Research Advisory Board of the Medical Research Future Fund, and was recognised as Australian of the Year in 2006. He was appointed Companion of the Order of Australia in the Queen's Birthday Honours list in 2013.

THE MEANING OF LIFE?

We are given only one life. While we may think we can influence how that life turns out, most of what happens between our birth and our death are outwith our immediate control. There is, in my opinion, no God out there, watching over us: rather, the laws of physics and chemistry determine our fate. However, these laws are not immutably defined: they involve probability/uncertainty, which we recognise by including the word 'quantum' in front of 'physics' and 'chemistry'.

Though we might like to believe otherwise, we have to accept that most of what we 'choose' to do, and what others choose for us to do, has remarkably little impact on other people's lives. The exceptions to this concept of 'little impact', whether good or bad, are generally recorded as history making, either within our social circle or, occasionally, on a local or global basis.

What does my view of the nature and purpose of life mean to me, as a doctor and a research scientist? Today, healthy, and comfortably off at the age of seventy, my thoughts are inevitably different from those I would have had fifty years ago, as an awkward recent graduate from self-centred adolescence, about to embark on training as a doctor. However, there are some constants. Much of my adult life has been driven by intellectual curiosity, somewhat impacted by the pleasures of social intimacy, self-challenge and creativity. Of these three pleasure drivers, creativity (by others) has given me the most satisfaction, probably because societal creativity, whether in music, the arts, science or medicine, tends to have lasting effects, and gives some sense of, if not immortality, at least a recognition after death.

I didn't set out to be creative. I was, as a twenty-year-old, quite hedonistic. Social intimacy, enjoyment of the outside world through travel and ski-ing, and enjoyment of the creativity of others in the arts, drove my life decisions, and they to some extent still do. However, somewhere in my mid twenties, I started to find satisfaction from providing service to others through health care delivery, though I think that my initial driver was curiosity about the nature of ill health, and the reasons why it occurred. This desire to understand, gradually changed into a desire to create new understanding, a change from 'what' to 'why'. It also introduced me to the pleasure to be had from puzzle solving, that, in retrospect, had led me as a child to doing jigsaws, and to taking things to bits to see how they worked. Creativity crept into the picture in my thirties with a desire to define the puzzle rather than just solve it, and focused my medical attention on to why some people were unlucky enough to get the diseases I was interested in, whereas most people did not.

As clinician scientists, we have defined, and continue to define, the medical puzzles presented by patients with health problems, recognising the importance of our genes, our environment and 'chance', though I'd now translate 'chance' back to quantum probability. I was lucky enough to be in the right place, and at the right time in history, to participate in the definition of the nature of, and a solution to, two problems of medical science – one led to better understanding of the nature of a particular cancer, and the other to a solution to prevent a particular cancer.

I recognise that I was fortunate to have met and have worked with people who gave me the opportunities and training that made it happen. So, while I'm recognised for what has been achieved through my discoveries, I recognise that credit is always more widely due than is publicly recognised and should be more widely shared. Helping others to participate in and benefit from all of life's pleasures and challenges, to the best of their ability, is in my opinion the true meaning of a meaningful life.

Ian Frazer AC, 22nd November 2023

'My thoughts are inevitably different from those I would have had fifty years ago.'

Dr MICHAEL IRWIN

DR MICHAEL IRWIN is a retired doctor and the former medical director of the United Nations. He has also worked as the UNICEF senior adviser on childhood disabilities, and the medical director for the World Bank and the IMF. He is a humanist and secular activist, campaigning in particular for voluntary euthanasia and doctor-assisted suicide. He served as the chairman of the Voluntary Euthanasia Society (now, renamed Dignity in Dying) and founded the Society for Old Age Rational Suicide (SOARS).

LIKE EVERYONE ELSE, I did not ask to be born. Like everyone else, I really have no definite idea why I am presently living on a tiny planet, rushing through this vast Universe. My father died at ninety. My mother at ninety-five. So, regarding longevity, I have good genes. However, now in my eighty-eighth year, while still enjoying this wonderful journey called 'Life', I am making preparations for my departure without causing myself, or anyone else, too much discomfort.

In Summer 2018, I am well aware that my increasingly decrepit body is getting to the stage when it will eventually be heavily dependent on others for its continuing existence. Of course, it is possible that I might die – from some presently undiagnosed condition (or the worsening of an existing disease) – before this happens. But, having had the good fortune to have, so far, a very 'Good Life', mainly in the Western world, I am now preparing for a very 'Good Departure'.

While everyone, as they age, usually focuses on how their bodies deteriorate, I have – for very many years – always considered that 'Michael Irwin' is basically my brain. Essentially, I am three pounds (or 1,400 grams) of billions of active nerve cells inside my skull – my brain is ME, my existence.

Every human brain is perhaps the most amazing grouping of cells in this amazing Universe. There are at least sixty billion neurons in the adult brain – this is seven times the number of people on Earth today.

Of course, my body is a vital part of who I am. It is what the rest of the world sees as 'me'. It is my obvious identity. It is the physical being that took me to work many years ago, and accompanied my brain to the theatre last month.

But, I am my brain. It is the source of all my thoughts and dreams. It studied to be a doctor, and then it worked in the 'UN System' for thirty-three years. It loved several wonderful women (and, lived with four of them). Like my parents' brains which created me, my brain was involved in being the father of three beautiful daughters. It campaigned for a sensible right-to-die law in the UK, and, getting to the end of a very satisfying existence on this unique planet, my brain is now preparing for a dignified departure – and, for perhaps discovering what might survive when my body ceases to exist.

The most fundamental questions of all, for those living on this planet, must surely be – 'Why is there something when there could be nothing?' 'Why am I here?' 'What happens when I die?' Of course, at present, we do not know the answers – but, we do usually realize that, on Earth, we are a very minute part of this amazing Universe.

The Universe is generally reckoned to be about 14 billion years old. Our galaxy – the Milky Way – has at least 100 billion stars (one of which is our sun) – yet, it is only one galaxy among perhaps 100 billion others.

Our Earth, travelling through space at some 67,000 miles an hour, only appeared about 4.5 billion years ago. Initially, there was no life at all on our planet. Eventually, single cell organisms apparently evolved from chemical reactions in the warm pools on the surface, and so the long road of evolution began, and is still continuing today (in fact, sometimes, I wonder how long the human thumb might eventually grow with so much texting and tweeting nowadays?).

On Earth, many thousands of species have developed in the past, and died. Dinosaurs existed for about 150 million years. Our earliest ancestors only appeared about 5 million years ago, eventually evolving into us, Homo sapiens, in the past 250,000 years.

If we can imagine that the history of all life on Earth is equal to the 365 days of one year – with each day representing 10 million years – then

Homo sapiens arrived about 11.30pm on December 31st. For those who believe in the existence of 'souls', I wonder when they think such entities entered our bodies during our extensive evolutionary process?

Our planet is a very small speck in this vast Universe. Yet on it, every creature that has ever lived – in the air, on the land, or in the ocean – has called it their home. Thinking only of humans, every emperor and peasant, every hero and coward, every father and mother, and every saint and sinner have existed on this tiny planet.

All living creatures are related – some, of course, are closer than others. Our human DNA is estimated to be 98.5% identical to that of a chimpanzee. Nine-tenths of our genes are similar to those of a mouse. And, at least a third of the genes of the lowly nematode worm is shared with us.

In our busy, daily lives, we tend to ignore the vastness of the Universe around us, and we easily forget that everyone is sentenced to die. Yet these two facts alone should remind us that our concerns and thoughts about our worldly possessions, about our regular ups and downs, should not really worry us too much – such matters are relatively insignificant, especially when measured against our destiny.

In the history of this Universe, our individual life is a momentary flicker. Our existence is for a relatively short period of time, basically between two periods of darkness. We arrive on Earth as a stranger, with no understanding of this world. We learn something of the ways of life here – and, like all visits, this one has its delights, its boredom and its ordeals. But, being a visit, our stay is limited.

Of course, there was a time, before we were born, when we did not exist. However, very few of us are concerned about this – especially as we have no memory of this.

So, why do so many of us, especially as we become old, worry about there being a time when we cease to exist as humans? Perhaps to die is simply to return to the state we were before we were born?

On the day that we do die, thousands and thousands of others, around the world, make the same journey. In the UK alone, about 600,000 people die every year. Every person one has ever met, everyone we pass on the street today, is going to die. Nearly the only thing that we can be certain of, in this life, is that one day, we will die, and leave everything behind us. We start to die once we are born – both are really natural events. Everyday, we travel towards our death, until, on our last day, we arrive at the terminal. We are all equal in having to face this eventuality. Thinking of chess, after the game, the king and the pawn go into the same box. Fortunately, we die only once. Therefore, it is surely wise to plan how we leave this existence?

Generally, in the Western world today, we shield people from death. In fact, we often avoid mentioning the word. Rather than say that someone has 'died', we use words like 'passed away', 'the departed' or, especially in speaking to children, 'joined the angels'. Nowadays, we make death as invisible as possible. The coffin is often closed. In fact, unlike past generations, we do not really know, or see, death any more – especially as it is more likely to occur in a hospital, a nursing home, or in a hospice, rather than at home (where, in fact, most people would prefer to die).

No one else can really share my perspective of this world. No one else can experience my feelings or have my consciousness. But, my life – one among some eight billion others on this tiny planet – is of momentous significance to me.

So, when I die, does my personal 'soul' enjoy an eternal reward – depending on how I have lived?

Or, am I going to be recycled or reincarnated (energy is never lost)? Or, do I totally disappear, snuffed out like a candle?

The idea of something surviving our earthly deaths has obvious appeal – or, is it just wishful thinking? One person who tried to prove the existence of a soul was Dr Duncan McDougall who, in 1907, at the Massachusetts General Hospital, in Boston, in America, constructed a bed mounted on a frame supported by platform beam scales 'sensitive to two-tenths of an ounce'. When he recorded the death of a terminally ill tuberculosis patient, he noticed that there was a sudden weight loss of 'precisely three-quarters of an ounce'. To my knowledge, this experiment has never been repeated!

I believe that there is some form of 'energy' – which exists in all living creatures – that enters at conception and leaves when we all die. How else to explain the essential difference between a living body and a dead one at the moment of death? There could easily be something that is still beyond the capacity of contemporary science, or the present laws of Nature, to explain. It is important not to fall into the trap of believing that what cannot be detected, at the present time, does not exist. Failure to find something is not evidence that it is not there.

In the first seven months of 2005, I contacted 1,600 individuals, picked at random from *Who's Who*, to obtain their views of what they thought survived when we died. When I analysed the 761 replies that I received – which I have been told was a very good response – I discovered that 46% believed that nothing at all survived death (except, of course, one's descendants, personal documents and photographs, etc); that 29% believed that a 'soul' continued to exist after death; and, 5% believed, like me, in the possibility of a non-specific 'life force' continuing to exist in some form after death. Only 20% were uncertain what survives when someone dies.

To be frankly honest, nobody on Earth today can be one hundred per cent certain of the answer. Life is a wonderful mystery, with so many possible answers. But, when death comes, the mystery might be gone for the one who dies. Upon dying, that individual might possibly know more about death than anyone presently on this planet. Perhaps for those of us alive, it is best to suspend absolute judgement, and refrain from either strongly believing or disbelieving? Although I presently do not believe it myself, if there is an afterlife, it is likely to be an even stranger existence than being born alive, on this planet. And, as I love having an issue for which one can campaign (like supporting the United Nations or seeking a right-to-die law), I wonder if I will be able to campaign there?

Professor
ANIL SETH

PROFESSOR ANIL SETH is professor of cognitive and computational neuroscience at the University of Sussex and director of the Sussex Centre for Consciousness Science. He is also co-director of the Canadian Institute for Advanced Research (CIFAR) Program on Brain, Mind, and Consciousness, a European Research Council (ERC) advanced investigator and editor-in-chief of the academic journal *Neuroscience of Consciousness* (Oxford University Press). His book *Being You: A New Science of Consciousness* was an instant *Sunday Times* Top 10 best-seller.

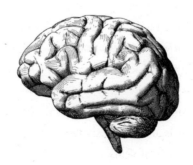

IT FEELS STRANGE to be writing to you about the meaning of life while my mother is struggling to hold onto hers. At the age of eighty-nine she's had a long life by the standards of human history, but any human life is the briefest glimmer in the vastness of time. The inconceivable brevity of human existence brings questions about meaning, purpose and fulfilment into sharp relief.

My mother was born in York in 1934, on Christmas Day, and grew up playing in the ruins of bombed-out buildings. She was a teacher, and later an artist and a landscape photographer. Lately, before her recent illness, she would wonder to me at the prospect of non-existence. She knows she will die, as most of us do at some level, but she cannot imagine not existing. As the horizons of her life have contracted, she has been able to find contentment in simpler and simpler things: the rhythms of the garden, the play of light on the leaves of a tree. This flexibility suggests to me that meaning, purpose and fulfilment are not only different things, but moving targets, if they are targets at all.

I've spent my career trying to understand more about the mystery of consciousness. About how the mess of neural wetware inside our heads can give rise to the everyday miracle of experience. Consciousness is intimately familiar to each of us. We all know what it's like to be conscious, and what it's like to lose consciousness when we fall into a dreamless sleep. The nature of consciousness is also endlessly perplexing, confounding scientists and thinkers for thousands of years.

Some people worry that pursuing a scientific perspective on

conscious experience might drain life of meaning by reducing us to mere biological machinery. I have found the opposite to be the case. There is no reduction. There is rather a continuity with the natural world, and with this continuity comes an expansion, a wider and deeper perspective. As we gradually pull back the curtains on the biological basis of conscious experience in all its richness, there are new opportunities to take ourselves and our conscious lives less for granted. We can see ourselves more as part of, and less apart from, the rest of nature. Our brief moments in the light of existence become more remarkable for having happened at all.

A recognition of the precarity of consciousness can help defuse some of our existential fears. We do not usually worry much about the oblivion that preceded our birth, so why should we worry about the equivalent oblivion that will follow our death? Oblivion isn't the experience of absence, it is the absence of experience. As the novelist Julian Barnes put it, in his meditation on mortality, there is 'nothing to be frightened of'.

I've come to think of consciousness as the precondition for meaning. An argument can be made that without consciousness, nothing would matter at all. Meaning, purpose and fulfilment can take many forms against this backdrop. The Aristotelian concept of eudaimonia best captures what I have in mind here. Eudaimonia means living well, flourishing, doing that which is worth doing. It is not about pleasure or hedonic satisfaction, nor is it about selfless sacrifice for some greater good. It involves realising one's potential through cultivating virtues such as reason, courage and wisdom. Fundamentally it comes down to doing a bit of good and feeling good about doing so.

For me, participating in some small way in the scientific and philosophical journey to understand ourselves and our place in nature, and communicating some of this journey to others, offers the promise of a slice of eudaimonia. In practice, frustration lurks at every turn. There is the risk of hubris when dealing with such apparently grand matters. And the dramas of everyday life get in the way.

Which brings me back to my mother. Today she has rallied, unexpectedly confounding the prognosis of the doctors. I asked her what she thought the meaning of life was, from her now frail vantage point. She told me it was about relationships with other people, and who can argue with that.

With best wishes

Anil

'We do not usually worry much about the oblivion that preceded our birth, so why should we worry about the equivalent oblivion that will follow our death?'

Sir TIM SMIT KBE

SIR TIM SMIT is the co-founder of the award-winning Eden Project near St Austell in Cornwall, UK. In 1987, Smit moved to Cornwall where he and John Nelson together 'discovered' and then restored the Lost Gardens of Heligan. He then turned his attention to regenerating a derelict clay-pit, and transformed it into a 'cradle of life containing world-class horticulture and startling architecture symbolic of human endeavour'. This became the award-winning Eden Project, which has welcomed more than nineteen million visitors since it opened in 2000. It aims to show humans are 'a part of nature, not apart from nature'. Eden Project International is now developing new projects across the UK and on every inhabited continent of the world.

I write this 40,000 ft above the Atlantic flying to America; two days have elapsed since my mother was laid to rest in an imprecisely deep grave in the medieval graveyard of St Ewe Church, near the Lost Gardens of Heligan in Cornwall.

It is an appropriate time to consider the importance or meaning of life. When young, I was infected with insatiable curiosity, so whether in good times or bad I retained the fervent desire to see tomorrow. As Mr Macawber famously believed in Charles Dickens' "Pickwick Papers" — Something will turn up.

More recently I have persuaded myself to try to become the person I wanted to be when I was young. Obviously the easy idealism has been infused with pragmatism but one with a heart of gold. I would advise against taking your life on the grounds that you'll die never knowing whether the dice of fate could roll in such a way that would transform you completely. If you die your future is, to a degree, certain. To live is to buy time to either improve yourself — or give yourself a better calling card in the here-after.

TLS.

I WRITE THIS 40,000 FEET above the Atlantic flying to America; two days have elapsed since my mother was laid to rest in an impossibly deep grave in the medieval graveyard of St Ewe Church near the Lost Gardens of Heligan in Cornwall.

It is an appropriate time to consider the importance or meaning of life. When young, I was infected with insatiable curiosity, so whether in good times or bad I retained the fervent desire to see tomorrow. As Mr Micawber famously believed in Charles Dickens' *Pickwick Papers* – something will turn up.

More recently I have persuaded myself to try to become the person I wanted to be when I was young. Obviously the easy idealism has been infused with pragmatism, but one with a heart of gold. I would advise against taking your life on the grounds that you'll die never knowing whether the dice of fate could roll in such a way that would transform you completely. If you die your future is, to a degree, certain. To live is to buy time to either improve yourself or give yourself a better calling card in the here-after.

'To live is to buy time to either improve yourself or give yourself a better calling card in the here-after.'

EDWARD O. WILSON

EDWARD O. WILSON (1929–2021) was an American biologist, naturalist and writer. His specialty was myrmecology, the study of ants, and he was nicknamed the 'ant man'. Wilson was the Pellegrino University Research Professor Emeritus in Entomology for the Department of Organismic and Evolutionary Biology at Harvard University, a lecturer at Duke University, and a fellow of the Committee for Skeptical Inquiry. He was a humanist laureate of the International Academy of Humanism, a two-time winner of the Pulitzer Prize for General Nonfiction and a *New York Times* best-selling author.

31 January 2018

Dear Mr. Bailey:

What an interesting question. It happens that I've recently written a book, *The Meaning of Human Existence*. The very short answer I'll give you here, if you don't find a better answer in my book is:

Each species alive is the supreme winner of a phylogenetic line of species that won the genetic competition among millions of other spsecies; each organism alive has done the same. Why destroy such a magnificent entity?

Best,

Edward O. Wilson

EOW:kmh

WHAT AN INTERESTING QUESTION. It happens that I've recently written a book, *The Meaning of Human Existence*. The very short answer I'll give you here, if you don't find a better answer in my book is:

Each species alive is the supreme winner of a phylogenetic line of species that won the genetic competition among millions of other species; each organism has done the same. Why destroy such a magnificent entity?

Dr MYA-ROSE CRAIG

DR MYA-ROSE CRAIG, also known as Birdgirl, is an ornithologist, author and campaigner for equal rights. She started her *Birdgirl Blog* in 2014, and in 2019 became the youngest person to see half of all the birds in the world. She founded the non-profit *Black2Nature* to help engage more children from minority ethnic backgrounds in conservation. Aged seventeen, she received an honorary doctorate in science from the University of Bristol, and is thought to be the UK's youngest recipient of the award.

I BELIEVE LIFE IS ABOUT LOVING and being loved. I grew up in a small close-knit family of myself, my sister Ayesha who was twelve years older than me, my dad Chris and mum Helena. Life was about the four of us, our love for each other, the hurdles that life threw at us and how, together, we were able to overcome them. Then came baby Laila, my niece, our number five, and my nephew, Lucas, our number six.

I never met either of my grandfathers as both died prematurely, leaving behind two big holes in our lives. Death shapes you and so did theirs.

The meaning of life for me started with the loss of these two amazing and loving people. The love from and for two people making my parents acutely aware that our time on earth was short and so every second counted.

We are a family of birdwatchers. Not just the kind that looks to the sky, but also the kind that treks up a far-off volcano for four days just for the chance of a glimpse of a critically endangered bird. This kind of passion and obsession is the glue holding us together and is the meaning of life for us. Everything points back to the 10,800 bird species that live on our planet and our determination to see every one.

Professor LORD ROBERT WINSTON

PROFESSOR LORD ROBERT WINSTON is Professor of Science and Society and Emeritus Professor of Fertility Studies at Imperial College. In the 1970s he developed gynaecological surgical techniques that improved fertility treatments. He later pioneered new treatments to improve *in vitro* fertilisation (IVF) and developed pre-implantation diagnosis. This allowed embryos to be screened for genetic diseases and has allowed parents carrying faulty genes to have children free of illnesses such as cystic fibrosis. He is a past chairman of the House of Lords Select Committee on Science and Technology, and also wrote and presented the BAFTA-winning show *The Human Body*.

Imperial College
London

Science and Society
Imperial College London

Professor Lord Winston F Med Sci, Hon FREng, DSc
Professor of Science and Society

22nd October 2015

Dear Mr Bailey

I really do not understand what you mean by the 'meaning of life'. To my mind life is a four-letter word and has a meaning, which is quite specific. But to talk about it in this kind of way argues some existential or philosophical meaning, which I have to admit I find somewhat pointless. I don't know why the meaning of life for a human life would be different from that of a whale or an ant, or indeed an oak tree. I don't think that there is such a meaning. What I do believe though, is that once we are alive (to misquote Dostoevsky's The Brothers Karamazov) we are responsible for everybody and everything which happens on the planet. But I have no idea whether that is the meaning of life.

Yours sincerely

Robert Winston.

Robert Winston

I REALLY DO NOT UNDERSTAND what you mean by the 'meaning of life'. To my mind life is a four-letter word and has a meaning, which is quite specific. But to talk about it in this kind of way argues some existential or philosophical meaning, which I have to admit I find somewhat pointless. I don't know why the meaning of life for a human life would be different from that of a whale or an ant, or indeed an oak tree. I don't think that there is such a meaning. What I do believe though, is that once we are alive (to misquote Dostoevsky's *The Brothers Karamazov*) we are responsible for everybody and everything which happens on the planet. But I have no idea whether that is the meaning of life.

Yours sincerely,
Robert Winston

'Life is a four-letter word.'

BILL McKIBBEN

BILL McKIBBEN is an author, environmentalist and activist. In 1988 he wrote *The End of Nature*, the first book for a common audience about global warming. He's gone on to write twenty books, and his work appears regularly in periodicals from the *New Yorker* to *Rolling Stone*. He serves as the Schumann Distinguished Scholar in Environmental Studies at Middlebury College, as a fellow of the American Academy of Arts and Sciences, and he has won the Gandhi Peace Prize. He co-founded 350.org, an international climate campaign, and is the founder of Third Act, which organises people over the age of sixty for action on climate and justice.

I'VE THOUGHT ABOUT THIS a good deal since you wrote.

I think the meaning of life is to keep the remarkable game of being human going forward. In the past this meant reproducing above all. But now it means, above all, preserving the board on which we play this game. And since we're now setting that board on fire, it's our job to put that fire out. In our time, that's the most important task we can undertake, since all depends on it. The best thing about the human game is that it, potentially, can stretch far out into the future – but only if we act now.

HENRY MARSH

CBE FRCS

HENRY MARSH is one of the UK's most eminent neurosurgeons. Until 2015, he was the senior consultant neurosurgeon at the Atkinson Morley Wing at St George's Hospital, London. Although retired from full-time work in the NHS, he continues to work in countries such as Ukraine, Nepal, Albania and Pakistan. His work in Ukraine was the subject of the documentary film *The English Surgeon*, which won an Emmy in 2010. His memoir *Do No Harm: Tales of Life, Death and Brain Surgery*, published in 2014, became an international best-seller. In 2023, he was awarded the Society of British Neurological Surgeons' medal for his outstanding contribution to neurosurgery.

TO TALK ABOUT 'the meaning of life' suggests that there is some kind of overall purpose over and beyond our daily lives. Although our scientific understanding of the physical world is very incomplete – it has, for instance, no explanation as to how physical matter gives rise to consciousness and perhaps never will – it has at least made teleology redundant. I prefer to talk about what gives life a sense of meaning – in other words, what means most to us in our lives, and that this can be understood in evolutionary terms. This is a personal question we each must answer for ourselves, and the answer will be different at the different stages of our lives. At the age of seventy-four with cancer (although currently in remission), it is quite clear to me that my family means most to me, followed by my writing and continuing work in medical education, especially in Ukraine, and finally my garden and woodworking. Looked at from an evolutionary perspective, these sources of meaning are the selfish propagation of my genes, the cooperation with others, tool-making and cultural accumulation that has been crucial to the 'success' of Homo sapiens, and the love of the natural world of which we are all part. It wasn't always like this – I was once an ambitious and competitive young surgeon, keen to succeed and to be seen, taking my family and the natural world for granted, and busy accumulating material possessions. I suppose that can be seen as the nest-building phase of my life. The world has changed since then – our exploitation of the natural world means that we are now precariously balanced on the edge of the precipice of war and catastrophic climate change.

It is easy to be wise in old age and in retrospect, but throughout my life I have always found that the greatest happiness in life is making others happy – at least, that all other pleasures are ephemeral in comparison. It is why it is such a privilege to be a doctor (although it comes at a price). But I have come to understand that 'others' includes all living things, whether sentient or not, although I must make an exception for bullies, various pathogenic organisms and for some of the weeds in my garden.

'At the age of seventy-four with cancer (although currently in remission), it is quite clear to me that my family means most to me.'

Dr KATHRYN MANNIX

DR KATHRYN MANNIX spent her medical career working with people who have incurable, advanced illnesses. Starting in cancer care and changing career to become a pioneer of the new discipline of palliative medicine, she has worked as a palliative care consultant in teams in hospices, hospitals and in patients' own homes, optimising quality of life, even as death is approaching. Her best-selling account of how people live while they are dying, *With the End in Mind*, was shortlisted for the Wellcome Prize, and her second book, *Listen: How to Find the Words for Tender Conversations*, was published in 2021.

EVERY MOMENT IS PRECIOUS – even the terrible moments. That's what I've learned from spending forty years caring for people with incurable illnesses, gleaning insights into what gives our lives meaning. Watching people living their dying has been an enormous privilege, especially as it's shown me that it isn't until we really grasp the truth of our own mortality that we awaken to the preciousness of being alive.

Every life is a journey from innocence to wisdom. Fairy stories and folk myths, philosophers and poets all tell us this. Our innocence is chipped away, often gently but sometimes brutally, by what happens to us. Gradually, innocence is transformed to experience, and we begin to understand who we are, how the world is, and what matters most to us.

The threat of having our very existence taken away by death brings a mighty focus to the idea of what matters most to us. I've seen it so many times, and even though it's unique for everyone, there are some universal patterns. What matters most isn't success, or wealth, or stuff. It's connection and relationships and love. Reaching an understanding like this is the beginning of wisdom: a wisdom that recognises the pricelessness of *this* moment. Instead of yearning for the lost past, or leaning into the unguaranteed future, we are most truly alive when we give our full attention to what is here, right now.

Whatever is happening, experiencing it fully means both being present and being aware of being present. The only moment in our lives that we can ever have any choice about is this one. Even then, we cannot choose our circumstances, but we can choose how we respond: we can rejoice in the good things, relax into the delightful, be intrigued by the unexpected, and we can inhabit our own emotions, from joy to fear to sorrow, as part of our experience of being fully alive.

I've observed that serenity is both precious and evanescent. It's a state of flow that comes from relaxing into what *is* without becoming distracted by what might follow. It's a state of mind that rests in appreciation of what we have rather than resisting it or disparaging it. The wisest people I have met have often been those who live the most simply, whose serenity radiates loving kindness to those around them, who have understood that all they have is this present moment.

That's what I've learned so far, but it's still a work in progress. Because it turns out that every moment of our lives is still a work in progress, right to our final breath.

'The wisest people
I have met have
often been those
who live the
most simply.'

DAME HILARY MANTEL

JULIAN FELLOWES

MICHAEL FRAYN FRSL

JODI PICOULT

ANTHONY HOROWITZ CBE

TONY WHEELER, AO

PICO IYER

GAYATRI CHAKRAVORTY SPIVAK FBA

AMOL RAJAN

SIR ALAN AYCKBOURN

SIMON CALDER

MONICA HEISEY

DONNA ASHWORTH

GYLES BRANDRETH

DANNY WALLACE

RUPI KAUR

Writers

Dame
HILARY MANTEL

DAME HILARY MANTEL (1952–2022) was the first female author to win the Booker Prize twice, which she did for the first two volumes in her epic trilogy of the life of Thomas Cromwell: *Wolf Hall* and *Bring Up the Bodies*. The novels, which have sold more than five million copies worldwide, were made into an acclaimed BBC series staring Mark Rylance, and adapted by Mantel herself for the RSC stage version. The trilogy culminated with *The Mirror and the Light*, which was also longlisted for the Booker Prize. Mantel wrote fourteen other celebrated books, and was awarded the National Book Critics Circle Award for Fiction, the Walter Scott Prize, the Costa Book Award, the Hawthornden Prize, and many other accolades.

Devon November 7th

Dear James,

I've had your letter for a fortnight, but I had to think about it a bit. You use two terms interchangeably: 'meaning' & 'purpose.' I don't think they're the same. I'm not sure life has a meaning, in the abstract. But it can have a definite purpose, if you decide so — and the carrying through, the effort to realise the purpose, makes the meaning for you.

It's like alchemy. The alchemists were on a futile quest, we think. There wasn't a philosophers' stone, & they couldn't make gold. But after many years of patience exercised, the alchemist saw he had developed tenacity, vision, patience, hope, precision — a range of subtle virtues. He had the spiritual gold, and he understood his life in the light of it. Meaning had emerged.

With my best wishes for your future —

Nick Hartley

I'VE HAD YOUR LETTER for a fortnight, but I had to think about it a bit. You use two terms interchangeably: 'meaning' and 'purpose'. I don't think they're the same. I'm not sure life has a meaning, in the abstract. But it can have a definite purpose if you decide so – and the carrying through, the effort to realise the purpose, makes the meaning for you.

It's like alchemy. The alchemists were on a futile quest, we think. There wasn't a philosopher's stone, and they couldn't make gold. But after many years of patience exercised, the alchemist saw he had developed tenacity, vision, patience, hope, precision – a range of subtle virtues. He had the spiritual gold, and he understood his life in the light of it. Meaning had emerged.

With very best wishes for your future.

Hilary Mantel

'I'm not sure life has a meaning, in the abstract. But it can have a definite purpose if you decide so.'

JULIAN FELLOWES

JULIAN FELLOWES, The Lord Fellowes of West Stafford, DL, is an actor, producer, novelist and screenwriter. He has received numerous accolades, including an Academy Award and two Emmy Awards, as well as nominations for four BAFTA Awards, a Golden Globe Award, two Olivier Awards and a Tony Award. Fellowes won the Academy Award for Best Original Screenplay for *Gosford Park*. He gained fame as the creator, writer and executive producer of the multiple award-winning ITV series *Downton Abbey* and the HBO series *The Gilded Age*. He also wrote the books for the Broadway musicals *Mary Poppins* (2006) and *School of Rock* (2015), and has authored two *Sunday Times* best-sellers, *Snobs* and *Past Imperfect*.

THANK YOU FOR YOUR LETTER which I'm afraid I have been rather slow in answering. I shall try my best.

Happiness is an elusive concept. There are of course moments in many lives – I would like to say 'most' but I might be pushing it a bit – where a person is flooded by the sensation of great and genuine happiness. It has certainly happened to me. But as a state of mind, I would suggest that 'contentment' is a more accurate representation of what we would consider a happy life. Are we content? And has what we have pursued throughout our lives made us content? That is the riddle.

To start with, I find that, when it comes to trying to assess what was the purpose of our lives, and whether it made us happy, I question now how much one is in control of these things. In my own case, I was very ambitious from an early age, and 'getting on' filled my thoughts, waking and sleeping, from when I first began to think at all. I had been badly bullied by one of my brothers throughout my childhood and this no doubt encouraged me in that 'I'll show them!' mentality, but my growing-up years were reasonably pleasant in other ways, my parents were loving and happy together, I never thought of us as rich, but of course we were rich, in comparison to ninety-eight per cent of the world's population, with our birthday cakes and ponies and trips to Switzerland and Spain.

With all this, I am not quite sure why I should have been so driven, but driven I was. Throughout those early years, I was permanently conscious of a desire to shine and because, in my youth, the shiniest people I was aware of were mainly movie stars, I wanted to be a movie star. The fact that

I was as plain as a pumpkin and with questionable talent was not allowed to deter me and, actually, proving the power of mind over matter, I did end up being moderately successful as an actor, a career for which I was not especially well equipped. By my forties, I was cast as a leading player by Danny Boyle in a mini-series for the BBC; I played in a Bond film and in films with Catherine Deneuve and Anthony Hopkins, when I am fairly sure others could have done a better job. I even had a running part in a popular series, only leaving, by my choice, in the fifth season, proving that an average performance backed by a determination that was almost unhinged could deliver on some level.

To be honest, I feel less of a fraud in my second career, as a writer, because here I think I did/do have a certain gift for a kind of drama, a sort of adult soap opera, emotional and funny, but not comedic, reinforced with a strongly visual element, that has found a surprising degree of popular support. But again, I feel this was all governed by my determination to succeed which came with my first signs of consciousness, rather than a proper artistic drive in search of creative fulfilment. And that determination has never really receded.

I say that, but I have changed in one way. When I was young, I did not understand people who lacked ambition. Men and women who were content with the cards they had been dealt and who placed more importance on their family life, or on serving the community in which they lived, in your terms on 'being happy'. I just didn't get it. But that has altered for me. Now, I look at people who lead modest, decent, hard-working lives, without the need for fame or fortune, and I understand the rewards of that choice. Indeed, I respect it, in a way that I never did before. I recognise it as a more dignified way of life than my own scramble for attention. But I have not changed so much that I would ever feel it could have been my path.

In a sense, writing gave me what I had been pursuing all that time, a degree of fame and fortune, as well as many other advantages, together with awards, including an Oscar which I had of course received many times in my youth in the form of a shampoo bottle, but which I ended up winning for real, all of which was the culmination of the dreams of my formative years and so the logical question is: Has all that made me happy? I would love to say yes. It has certainly not made me unhappy. But the truth of burning ambition is that the fire never completely goes out. There is still more you can do, more you can gain, and so I do not find it easy to believe I will ever be allowed to rest, pleasantly cushioned, reading a book, in a state called happiness.

Thankfully, I have been very lucky in my private life, having spent thirty-four years with my excellent and even unique wife, Emma, and I am thrilled by, and proud of, the achievements of our son, Peregrine, so all of that may be counted as happy, indeed the two of them have probably given me the nearest to the state of happiness that I will ever get, even if I suspect the hounds of ambition will be snapping at my heels until I have completed the journey.

In conclusion, all I would say is that the approach of old age – I will be seventy-five this year – has encouraged a certain generosity towards others that I am not sure was there from the start. I know now I will probably always need to be involved in some project or other, if only in a supervisory capacity, but I watch my son and his contemporaries moving forward in their chosen careers and I am glad for them. Some of my generation have trouble with the fact that the moving finger writes and then moves on, but I don't. I've had a lot of success and enjoyed it, and now it's their turn. I suppose that, in making that admission, I must have found a kind of contentment with the way of the world, after all.

Yours ever,
Julian
The Lord Fellowes of West Stafford, DL

MICHAEL FRAYN FRSL

MICHAEL FRAYN is an acclaimed playwright and novelist. His plays include *Copenhagen*, *Democracy* and *Donkeys' Years*. His novels, such as *Towards the End of the Morning*, *Headlong* and *Spies*, have also been critical and commercial successes, making him one of the handful of writers in the English language to succeed in both drama and prose fiction. Frayn is perhaps best known for his long-running, internationally successful stage farce *Noises Off*, a frenetic play-within-a-play about the antics of an English theatrical company.

THANK YOU FOR INVITING ME to contribute to your anthology of views on the meaning of life. It's not something I can respond to, I'm afraid, because it's not clear to me how 'life' can have a 'meaning' in any ordinary sense of either word. It might be an idea to start with something smaller, say a pickled walnut. Once we've got it clear how a pickled walnut could have a 'meaning', we might move on to something larger – the Borough of Haringey, say, or influenza – and work our way up.

Michael Frayn

'It might be an idea to start with something smaller, say a pickled walnut.'

JODI PICOULT

JODI PICOULT is the #1 *New York Times* best-selling author of twenty-nine novels, including *Small Great Things*, *Wish You Were Here* and *My Sister's Keeper*, which was adapted into a movie starring Cameron Diaz. Approximately forty million copies of her books are in print worldwide, translated into thirty-four languages. In her novels, Picoult has covered a wide range of controversial or moral issues, including abortion, assisted suicide, race relations, eugenics, LGBT rights, fertility issues, religion, the death penalty and school shootings.

Apologies for the brief note, James — to me the meaning of life is the measure of how many minds you have opened in your wake. From your own family to the minds of strangers — what are you doing in your brief existence to make the world a more equitable place for all?

x Jodi Picoult

APOLOGIES FOR THE BRIEF NOTE, James – to me the meaning of life is the measure of how many minds you have opened in your wake. From your own family to the minds of strangers – what are you doing in your brief existence to make the world a more equitable place for all?

ANTHONY HOROWITZ CBE

ANTHONY HOROWITZ is a novelist who has written over fifty books. His best-selling teen spy Alex Rider series is estimated to have sold twenty-one million copies worldwide and has been turned into a movie and a TV series. He is also an acclaimed writer for adults and was commissioned to write two new Sherlock Holmes novels, and commissioned by the Ian Fleming Estate to write continuation novels for James Bond. Horowitz's award-winning novel *Magpie Murders* was serialised on BritBox with Lesley Manville in the lead role.

STORMBREAKER
P R O D U C T I O N S

ANTHONY HOROWITZ, OBE

30 November 2017

Dear Mr Bailey,

Thank you for your interesting letter.

I think it is very hard to find meaning, purpose or fulfilment in life because life is so very messy, difficult...and short. It's why I've always disliked religion which tries to find "big" answers to questions that really it's better not to ask. But I do experience moments of perfect happiness...a cup of tea and a chocolate biscuit after a long walk with my dog might be one of them. Not profound, perhaps, but immaculate. It's the small pleasures that keep me going – and you have to be alive to enjoy them.

I hope this helps.

Best wishes,

THANK YOU FOR YOUR INTERESTING LETTER.

I think it's very hard to find meaning, purpose or fulfilment in life because life is so very messy, difficult . . . and short. It's why I've always disliked religion which tries to find 'big' answers to questions that really it's better not to ask. But I do experience moments of perfect happiness . . . a cup of tea and a chocolate biscuit after a long walk with my dog might be one of them. Not profound, perhaps, but immaculate. It's the small pleasures that keep me going – and you have to be alive to enjoy them.

I hope this helps.

Best wishes,

Anthony Horowitz

'It's the small pleasures that keep me going – and you have to be alive to enjoy them.'

TONY WHEELER, AO

TONY WHEELER is a publishing entrepreneur, travel writer and the co-founder, with his wife Maureen Wheeler, of the Lonely Planet guidebook company. After travelling across Europe, the couple arrived in Melbourne in 1972 and put out their first book, *Across Asia on the Cheap,* in 1973. This would grow into the Lonely Planet empire. In the 2014 Queen's Birthday Honours List, Wheeler was appointed an Officer of the Order of Australia, for 'distinguished service to business and commerce as a publisher of travel guides, and as a benefactor to a range of Australian arts and aid organisations'.

THE MEANING OF MY LIFE.

It's a little late for me to try and do something really useful now, I have to live with what my life has been. I'm not going to make any big changes – now – in the years I have left. Next lifetime, well I'll do things differently, starting with putting more effort into languages. OK I can ask for a cold beer – *cerveza fría* – *bir dingin* – *kaltes bier* – in a surprising number of languages, but after that my linguistic abilities rapidly fade. But even in that next lifetime I don't see myself doing anything wonderful politically, socially, culturally, so I'll just have to live with what my life has been and still is. And that comes down to one word: 'travel'.

At this end of my life, in our much battered world as it is today, saying that travel is what your life has been all about has to immediately be defended – what about climate change, over-tourism, all those terrible negative effects of travel? Shouldn't I just be retreating indoors, shutting the door, going nowhere and in that way making a tiny baby step towards righting all the damage I've done in my lifetime? Sure I could, or I could put the next thousand words into defending the positive side of travel, that it's how we meet the world, that it employs so many people, that it's not any worse than lots of other ways we can damage our environment from addiction to fast fashion to mining crypto-currencies. So I am not going to bother.

The simple reality has been that my working life has been all about travel and even now, well past the end of my working life and sliding down what is clearly going to be my final years, travel is what I love most. In fact my travel addiction started even before my working years: as a child the whole idea of going somewhere, seeing places, clearly had a fascination whether it was collecting stamps, drawing maps or even asking for a globe as a Christmas present. Then in my late school years, at university, I started travelling and not much later I found a way to turn an attraction into an occupation and a lifetime story: Lonely Planet.

That very first guidebook, an amateurish affair exactly fifty years old as I write this, was an accident. I didn't set out on the hippie trail – the Asia overland route as we defined it at the time – intending to make a career out of it. Lots of other young people, baby boomers like me, were doing the same trip and to be quite honest many of them made a far better job of it than I did. They travelled further, longer, more adventurously, with more understanding, than I ever did. Tough luck, they didn't make a generational pursuit out of their great trip, I did.

Fifty years after that very first guidebook it's hardly surprising that I'm regularly being asked to look back at what we helped to create, because from the very start it was two of us, my wife Maureen and I, not a solo endeavour. And I am proud of it, as I've already confessed travel is not an unmitigated good, there are considerable downsides, but overall I think the travel revolution that has taken place during my lifetime has been a wonderful force for good. It's not only 'us' going out into the world and meeting 'them' it has also been the other way around, the world bouncing back to engage with us.

I've seen that in all sorts of ways, close to home (or close to the business) I regularly meet up with the writers, researcher, editors, cartographers who put those guidebooks together and without exception they're still amazingly enthusiastic about what they helped to create. 'The best job of my life' is a line I've regularly heard, quickly followed by wonderful stories of adventurous trips, of incredible encounters, of all the experiences that can make travel so important. And on the other side of the picture, the people who have used those guidebooks, who have gone out to enjoy their own travelling adventures, have simply been astonishingly generous in their comments, praise, thanks for what I helped to produce over a fifty-year time span.

And in between, I love the stories of people we've crossed paths with. Hotel owners in developing world regions who we praised, and thereby helped their businesses, who have gone on to prove that their view of the world has been the right one. People who, at great personal cost, kept their employees on the payroll through the depressions of the pandemic, for example. Or people who have gone on to do 'good things' outside their own business, who have on the side supported health and educational projects. We've been fortunate enough to be able, in our turn, to support their projects. My travel story has been financially successful and I don't need possessions and trophies to show for that, it's been far more satisfying to put resources into worthwhile projects. My own travels are often punctuated by dropping in to schools, or hospitals, or scientific projects, or even refugee camps, to check out where we have done our tiny little bit of good.

But profession, philanthropy and everything else apart, the simple fact is that I love to travel. I love to see new places, to discover the history, the artefacts, the culture, the back story behind so much of our world. I've often said that my favourite place in the world is the departure lounge, because then I know I'm on my way somewhere. Although equally my favourite means of transport are still my own two feet or a bicycle.

PICO IYER

PICO IYER is an essayist and the author of sixteen books, on subjects ranging from the Dalai Lama to globalism, from the Cuban Revolution to Islamic mysticism. They include such long-running sellers as *Video Night in Kathmandu*, *The Lady and the Monk*, *The Global Soul*, *The Open Road* and *The Art of Stillness*. He has also written regularly for *Time*, the *New York Times*, the *New York Review of Books*, the *Financial Times* and more than 250 other periodicals worldwide. Since 1992, Iyer has spent much of his time at a Benedictine hermitage in Big Sur, California, and most of the rest in suburban Japan.

'**WHEN PEOPLE SAY THEY WISH** to find the meaning of life, what they're really looking for is a deep experience of life.' Thirty-seven years on, I can never forget the words of Joseph Campbell, unstoppably vigorous in his eighty-third year, speaking to twenty of us seven months before his death. Any meaning that could be summarized is one I would not trust, or feel could not be adequate, like reducing a slant of light to syllables; but any moment that releases me from speech – from time, from care, even from myself – is probably so essential that it saves me from ever having to worry about either meaning or life.

I have found such transport – effectively a dissolving of self – in two ways: through the writing that is my daily practice, and through the silence I enter whenever I go on retreat. Anyone who does it for a living knows that writing is much of the time the most impossible, frustrating, wearying task imaginable, a lover who turns her back on you and refuses to say a word. But none of that diminishes the many times when it is pure joy, the greatest adventure around, precisely because I am out of myself, giving voice to something far wiser than I could ever be. Something comes out of me that I never knew was inside of me, and the writing makes me far more than the other way round.

The first time I went to spend three days in a Benedictine hermitage, I worried that it would feel strange – or I would – because I'm not a Christian. The moment I stepped into the silence of my cell there, every doubt disappeared – as did every anxiety, dogma and battle I had been entertaining on the long drive up. Silence belongs to all of us, I realized, and speaks to us at some level deeper than any text or doctrine. And in that pulsing silence, found to some degree in any convent or monastery, within any order – an active, living silence (not just the absence of noise) – I felt empty and full all at once. Empty of myself, and my tiny plans, full of the much more radiant and enduring things all around me: the rabbit in my garden, the light upon the fence, the sun on the ocean far below.

Ironically, in both activities, what I claimed was solitude, the chance to be alone, in intimate contact with the world, and with whatever depths I far too often misplace. But as I began to return to silence – I've made more than a hundred retreats in that same monastery, over thirty-two years now – I came to see that solitude is merely a means to better understanding community and compassion. I was never less alone than when sitting in that empty, silent cell. And all the people I care for felt closer to me, more vibrant – more enchanted – than if they'd been standing across the room.

Silence taught me, in other words, much as writing does, that the meaning of life comes in the sharing of it with others. But sometimes I have to be alone – at my desk, or in my room above the sea – to be able to collect or recollect all that I long to pass on to everyone else. It doesn't matter whether your practice is dancing or painting, cooking or playing the violin; the meaning comes when you leave yourself behind and reach out towards everybody else.

'It doesn't matter whether your practice is dancing or painting, cooking or playing the violin; the meaning comes when you leave yourself behind and reach out towards everybody else.'

GAYATRI CHAKRAVORTY SPIVAK FBA

GAYATRI CHAKRAVORTY SPIVAK is an Indian-American scholar, literary theorist and feminist critic. She is a professor at Columbia University and a founding member of the establishment's Institute for Comparative Literature and Society. Considered one of the most influential postcolonial intellectuals, Spivak was awarded the 2012 Kyoto Prize in Arts and Philosophy and the Padma Bhushan, one of India's highest honours, in 2013.

Dear Mr. Bailey:

For me life means itself. I like recognition. I do what I do because I'm driven. If asked, I say my purpose is to continue social justice indefinitely into the future. In fact, my "purpose" seems to be dictated from calls that come from outside.
I hope this suffices. Thank you for including me in your august list,

Gayatri Chakravorty Spivak

[signature]
1/19/18

FOR ME LIFE MEANS ITSELF. I like recognition. I do what I do because I'm driven. If asked, I say my purpose is to continue social justice indefinitely into the future. In fact, my 'purpose' seems to be dictated from calls that come from outside.

I hope this suffices.
Gayatri Chakravorty Spivak
1/19/18

AMOL RAJAN

AMOL RAJAN is a journalist, broadcaster and writer. He worked as an adviser to Lord Lebedev of Siberia, and was appointed the editor of his newspaper the *Independent* in 2013. He became the BBC's first media editor in 2016, and has been a presenter on the *Today* programme on BBC Radio 4 since 2021. He has presented on BBC Radio 2 and, in 2023, he replaced Jeremy Paxman as the host of *University Challenge*.

Dear James (if I may), Thank you very much indeed for your letter (date unknown) about the meaning of life. I don't know if life has a particular meaning. We are the product of evolutionary forces that inspire awe. But I do think life has value. That value can be found by searching for true knowledge, feeling the suffering of our fellow souls, and enjoying the love of those we most treasure. Best of luck with your wonderful project.

DEAR JAMES (IF I MAY), Thank you very much indeed for your letter (date unknown) about the meaning of life. I don't know if life has particular meaning. We are the product of evolutionary forces that inspire awe. But I do think life has value. That value can be found by searching for true knowledge, feeling the suffering of our fellow souls, and enjoying the love of those we most treasure. Best of luck with your wonderful project.

Sir ALAN AYCKBOURN

SIR ALAN AYCKBOURN is a highly successful and prolific British playwright and director. He has written and produced more than eighty full-length plays and was, between 1972 and 2009, the artistic director of the Stephen Joseph Theatre in Scarborough, where all but four of his plays have received their first performance. More than forty have subsequently been produced in the West End, at the Royal National Theatre or by the Royal Shakespeare Company since his first hit, *Relatively Speaking*, opened at the Duke of York's Theatre in 1967. His plays have won numerous accolades, including seven London Evening Standard Awards. Ten of his plays have been staged on Broadway, attracting two Tony nominations and one Tony Award. Ayckbourn has also been honoured with Laurence Olivier (2009) and Tony (2010) Awards for lifetime achievement.

25th November 2017

Dear James Bailey,

What a fascinating project.

Sixty years ago with a burgeoning acting career on the verge of being a professional playwright and director, I would probably have readily answered your question. I felt, as they say, that the world was at my feet. These days, alas, I sense very much it is on my back. I have no idea why I write nor indeed why I'm still alive. Probably the writing is as much a reflex for me as breathing. That's all I can say.

Sorry but you caught me at the wrong end of my existence. My brief answer: What the hell?

Best wishes,

Yours sincerey,

Alan Ayckbourn

Westborough
Scarborough
North Yorkshire
YO11 1JW

Administration
01723 370540

Box Office
01723 370541

Fax
01723 360506

enquiries@sjt.uk.com

www.sjt.uk.com

Scarborough Theatre Trust Ltd.
Reg. No. 815227 (England)
Reg. Charity No. 253606

WHAT A FASCINATING PROJECT.

Sixty years ago with a burgeoning career on the verge of being a professional playwright and director, I would probably have readily answered your question. I felt, as they say, that the world was at my feet. These days, alas, I sense very much it is on my back. I have no idea why I write nor indeed why I'm still alive. Probably the writing is as much a reflex for me as breathing. That's all I can say.

Sorry but you caught me at the wrong end of my existence. My brief answer: What the hell?

Best wishes,

Yours sincerely,

Alan Ayckbourn

'My brief answer: What the hell?'

SIMON CALDER

SIMON CALDER is a travel journalist and broadcaster. Calder's first job was a cleaner for British Airways at Gatwick airport. He later worked as a security guard frisking passengers. It was during the long gaps between flights that he began to write budget travel guidebooks, starting with the *Hitch-hiker's Manual: Britain*. He has since researched and written guides to Amsterdam, Cuba, the Americas and Eastern Europe. He became travel correspondent for the *Independent* in 1994 – a position he holds to this day – and since then he has travelled to more than 120 countries, flown on Concorde, travelled on the Trans-Siberian Railway and provided his travel expertise on countless TV shows.

SINCE LIFE ON EARTH FIRST EVOLVED in the form of microbes about four million years ago, the meaning of life has been simple: a pre-ordained duty to reproduce, with grim determination.

Yet evolution has delivered those with the immense fortune to be living in a relatively wealthy, liberal and democratic nation in the third decade of the twenty-first century with the best possible hand. We can choose not to reproduce and to watch Netflix instead, while eating and drinking on the best the world can offer. Better still, we can travel. Human evolution favours exploration: to discover new lands that can support people, and to widen the gene pool. These days, though, the main driver for many of us is self-enrichment: to widen our eyes and our minds with experiences of different lands, cultures and cuisines.

No previous generation has enjoyed such limitless horizons: the chance to travel in greater safety, at lower cost, to the ends of the earth (and, these days, beyond). Many will find fresh meaning in their lives as a result. When luckier, richer citizens travel to poorer nations, they transfer wealth effortlessly. Tourism creates jobs and improves international understanding.

Blaise Pascal, the French mathematician and philosopher, mourned: 'All the unhappiness of men arises from one single fact, that they cannot stay quietly in their own chamber.' *Au contraire*: humanity's ability to venture far and wide – to learn what binds us together – is evolution's greatest achievement.

MONICA HEISEY

MONICA HEISEY is an author, essayist and screenwriter. She began her writing career contributing to publications including the *Guardian*, the *New Yorker* and the *New York Times*. Since then she has worked on television projects including *Schitt's Creek*, *Workin' Moms*, *The Cleaner* and *Everything I Know About Love*. As a member of the writing room for the sketch comedy series *Baroness von Sketch Show*, she was awarded four Canadian Screen Awards for comedy writing. Her debut novel *Really Good, Actually* was published in 2023, and her comedy series *Smothered* premiered on Sky.

YOURS IS A BIG QUESTION, certainly, and one I have been thinking about a lot this year. Last spring my niece Rosemary was born, squirming and healthy and pink, with my sister's big blue eyes and my brother-in-law's button nose. Nine days later, she died in her sleep. On the phone with my sobbing mother, I realized my sense of life's meaning had been undefined, or at least had never been tested. I'd been chugging along, untouched by capital-T tragedy, oblivion feeling blissfully abstract. Confronted for the first time with the Real Deal, I searched for meaning, and found none. There had been no warning, would turn out to be no cause, and of course it had not happened 'for a reason'. Something terrible had occurred from nowhere, and now our lives were changed forever, and Rosie would not get to have one. I felt nihilism like a rip tide, swirling around me and tugging at my ankles. It would have been easy to go under.

But the days and weeks after the meaningless cruelty of Rosie's death also taught me about life's purpose, or at least showed me a way I might define it. I had anticipated a week of quiet mourning punctuated by a kind of depressed chaos as everyone scrambled to arrange a funeral and perform grim and foreign administrative tasks. I assumed tragedy on this scale would feel lonely. But my memories from that period are densely populated: old friends rallying, travelling long distances to hold my sister and her husband and look at pictures and remember a person they would never get to know; my long-divorced parents coming together to provide a soft place to land for their three long-grown children; distant relatives with stories we'd never heard about cousins we'd also never be able to meet; a cluster of colleagues surrounding my sister, huddling like a football team about to break for a challenging second half; the unlikely presence of my divorce lawyer with a box of homemade scones and clotted cream. Instead of numb or adrift, I felt almost painfully alive. We were surrounded, I realized, by Rosie's community, who were of course ours too. There were faces I hadn't seen in years – due to life and geography and the pandemic – and I saw then that they had not been gone, not really. We hadn't 'lost touch', we had just been busy, all of us, with work and children and the business of living, but now they were needed, and so here they were. Increasingly I think this is the only purpose we have: to be in connection with each other, to batten down our collective hatches against life's many and various brutalities. Everything else that feels like purpose, to me – making and consuming art, engaging in collective efforts to better society or the planet, listening deeply to loved ones – is really an avenue to connection, providing it and being enriched by it, too.

In terms of happiness, many people more intelligent than I have suggested shooting for contentment instead, and I think they are right. Still, there are some things that make me reliably happy, and I have found much contentment in cultivating opportunities to experience them. These include: friends' laughter, reading at the bar, unrealistically flattering denim, good gossip, morning sex, coffee and a walk with a slight hangover, a sunny day experienced from a safely shaded area, cornbread, cats, the exhilaration of being bad at something new, boxing (relatedly), and making a sauce for three to five hours. There are more, of course – the list grows all the time – and keeping track of them feels important. I suppose happiness is knowing what is personally meaningful to you, and engaging with it, which is kind of a nice full circle to come to in this letter. A natural conclusion that returns to the beginning makes me happy, too. Another for the list.

All my best,
Monica

'I think this is the only purpose we have: to be in connection with each other, to batten down our collective hatches against life's many and various brutalities.'

DONNA ASHWORTH

DONNA ASHWORTH is a two-times *Sunday Times* best-selling poet who is known for her motivational content for mental and emotional health. Her writing came to the spotlight during the Covid lockdown period, where she saw her purpose as building a place to find hope, calm and comfort, amidst the collective chaos. Her latest book, *Wild Hope*, aspires to help us find hope, peace, self-acceptance and inspiration on the days we feel worn down, helpless or sad.

THE MEANING OF LIFE

The meaning of life?
To me, is clear
that the reason for all of it,
the why we are here . . .
is everything.
The fingerprints only you can bring,
the way your growth aligns with spring
and retreats, to sleep,
with winter.
Each of us a sparkling splinter,
of universe,
unique and diverse.
Yet of the same.
We all gather to play this game,
then forget why we came.
And I blame thinking,
when we should be linking,
fingers together and arms around trees.
Not letting the rat-race bring us to our knees
we seek peace,
a sweet release.
But we look in wrong places,
we search for traces,
of ourselves,
in bottomless wells.
Such tales we tell,
of heaven and hell
but I think they exist
in our hearts
perhaps not worlds apart,
after all.
The meaning of life?
Lives in the small.

GYLES BRANDRETH

GYLES BRANDRETH is a writer, broadcaster, actor and former MP. His many books include an acclaimed childhood memoir, *Odd Boy Out*, as well as nine detective novels (among them *The Oscar Wilde Murder Mysteries*), biographies (notably *Elizabeth: An Intimate Portrait*, and *Philip: The Final Portrait*) and three other recent best-sellers: *The 7 Secrets of Happiness*; a celebration of good English, punctuation, spelling and grammar, *Have You Eaten Grandma?*; and his anthology of poetry to learn by heart, *Dancing by the Light of the Moon*.

WHEN I WAS ABOUT TEN OR ELEVEN, my headmaster, Mr Stocks, gave me what he said was his best advice. 'Brandreth,' he said, 'remember this: busy people are happy people.'

That's been my philosophy of life ever since and it has served me well. It's also enabled me to find time to write a little book called *The 7 Secrets of Happiness* and if I was going to answer your letter properly, I would simply send you a copy of that book! In fact, if you manage to find a copy, do feel free to quote anything from it.

With best wishes,

Gyles

PS. When I was in my teens, I embarked on a similar project to yours and I recall that one of the people I wrote to was Field Marshal Montgomery. He sent me a wonderful reply that you might like to quote in your book. I put it in my book *Odd Boy Out* – but unfortunately I seem to have given all my copies away and I can't find one to quote the quotation for you! If you manage to get hold of the book, do look up Montgomery in the index and see what I am talking about.

DANNY WALLACE

DANNY WALLACE is a *Sunday Times* best-selling author, as well as a BAFTA-, Arqiva- and Sony-winning performer and presenter. His first book, *Join Me*, explained how Wallace 'accidentally started a cult'. His second book, *Yes Man* – in which he decided to say 'Yes' to everything – became a hugely successful film with Jim Carrey in the lead role. He has written and presented shows on all the major UK television and radio networks, and he currently presents the Important Broadcast on Radio X.

I DON'T KNOW what the meaning of life is. The things decent people find most meaning in involves being decent.

I think that's a clue.

But if I had to guess, I think the meaning of life for most of us – both decent or non-decent or indecent – could be in the minuscule discoveries and small moments that happen between the big ones we're all supposed to find so life-changing.

Your instinct is to say that the most important moments of your life have to be the huge ones, and that any shift has almost to be world-changing, but what if life is not about changing the world but changing enough of its small moments . . .

Maybe a moment so small it's just between you and a cat on the street.

Where you and the cat are the only witnesses to it ever happening at all.

And neither of you – especially not the cat – will ever tell another soul?

Maybe you improve her day ever-so-slightly with a stroke of the ear or a lift-up to wherever she needs to be to find the sun.

Maybe you sit with her a moment, or maybe it's her that sits with you.

And from the glance she gives you, that glance you know is appreciation, you've made a connection between two things as different as a pin and a bicycle. And you remember the feeling of peace and purring and connection.

No one else needs to know about it. It's almost not worth mentioning. But it happened and it was good.

Maybe there's no grand plan or meaning to life at all, unless we think of life as something that every so often, if we accept, offers us a few wonderful seconds of meaning we will struggle to recall but never really forget.

Between you and a cat. A partner. A friend. A child you hope in some way remembers those times you lifted her up to wherever she needed to be to find the sun.

And that's not bad, right?

'What if life is not about changing the world but changing enough of its small moments ...'

RUPI KAUR

RUPI KAUR is a Canadian poet, artist and performer. A breakout literary phenomenon and #1 *New York Times* best-selling author, she wrote, illustrated and self-published her first poetry collection, *milk and honey*. Her follow-ups, *the sun and her flowers* and *home body*, both debuted at #1 on best-seller lists across the world. These collections have sold over twelve million copies and have been translated into over forty languages, with *milk and honey* becoming one of the highest-selling poetry books of the twenty-first century. In 2021, Kaur produced *Rupi Kaur Live*, a first-of-its-kind poetry special on Amazon Prime Video. Kaur also executive produced the film *This Place*, which premiered at the Toronto International Film Festival in 2022, and the 2024 Academy Award–nominated film *To Kill a Tiger*. Kaur has graced stages across the globe and completed her third sell-out world tour in 2023.

- laughing
- dancing
- expressing myself
- learning to love
- star gazing
- making my parents smile
- relishing pastries
- empathy, compassion, and seva
- witnessing nature
- feeling connected
- releasing the old and embracing the new
- trusting what the future will bring
- falling in love with myself

RUPI KAUR

- laughing
- dancing
- expressing myself
- learning to love
- stargazing
- making my parents smile
- relishing pastries
- empathy, compassion, and seva
- witnessing nature
- feeling connected
- releasing the old and embracing the new
- trusting what the future will bring
- falling in love with myself

SUSAN POLLACK MBE

MARTINE WRIGHT MBE

SIMON WESTON CBE

MIKE HAINES OBE

NATALIE QUEIROZ MBE

SIR TERRY WAITE KCMG CBE

CHRIS MOON MBE

MATT LEWIS

BRIAN CLARK

JOHN HOSKISON

Survivors & Campaigners

SUSAN
POLLACK MBE

SUSAN POLLACK is a Holocaust survivor. Following the outbreak of the Second World War, her family were sent by cattle truck to Auschwitz-Birkenau. Pollack was selected to work and remained in the camp for around ten weeks before being sent to Guben in Germany to work as a slave labourer in an armaments factory. With the Allies advancing, the prisoners were forced on a death march to Bergen-Belsen. On 15 April 1945, Pollack was liberated by the British army. After she was hospitalised for tuberculosis, typhoid and severe malnutrition, she was sent to Sweden to recover. More than fifty of her relatives were killed during the Holocaust. Pollack now lives in London, and works with the Holocaust Educational Trust to share her testimony about the horrors that occurred during the Second World War.

17th Feb 2018   1.)

Dear Mr. James Bailey,

In response to your letter enquiry, here are a few thoughts that assisted me to look forward, in my youth after those bleak, horrendous times in 1945. I am a camp survivor from Auschwitz and liberated in Belgen Belsen on the 15th April 1945. I was totally dehumanized, fearful distrustful. Lost to contemplate the future. All alone, unable to comprehend the values for a life in a modern civilization. Being brought up in a village in Hungary, removed from the sophistication of a "new world" how can I find myself - trusting others without a voice, unable to articulate any latent desires, that gradually emerged - that did not include me, with no one listening.

       Fourteen years old - unable to walk, to express the latent, supressed anguish - the realization I only speak Hungarian, no skills, no education, no finance, no support system, no knowledge.

The first great awareness discovery in Belgen Belsen was the discovery that kindness and goodwill has also survived. When the British soldier lifted me up from the mud hole - seeing a towel in my body - he gently placed me in one of the small ambulances. That experience - miraculous goodwill is one of the guiding lights to this day I often think of that moment and ask "What part

141

that Goodness into your heart you battle
worn soldier ?"

Kindness, generosity, comes in small
everyday events. Small measures of goodness
has an enormous impact – to this day I
take nothing for granted – remember the effect
and appreciation this first helpfulness had on
my life – It gradually removed the heavy
iron cover off me and sparks of I can do
and want to do gradually came into my
existence.

In Sweden where I was taken for recuperation
after my devastated physical corpse-like being,
one of the facilitators had a large collection of
classical records. these he played every evening
and we sat and listened in awe to Beethoven
symphonies and other pieces. In my interpretation
I could feel the energy of rebirth from sorrow
and despair to the drive of supreme human
effort to rise above those distinctive memories.
I must say not completely – Personally I do not
want to let it go completely – but I am free of
the chains which deprived me in the camps.
Music generally has an enormous effect of my
life – I moved on. I became a Samaritan helper
"can I help you?" for some 4 years.

3.) I took a degree at the age of 60 years —
And then a diploma in Paperology —

For me life is full of possibilities, like a
search engine — find your meaning for existance
that makes me feel worthy — self esteem is the reward.

I was fortunate in having a family and could
play with my grandchildren. ~~reliving~~ those lost
years of persecution. reclaiming

I remember the the doctor in Sweden who
took me on his arms to teach me walking
and turned to me saying "I have a little
girl like you" What a discovery about myself —
Powerful words that still rings in my ears
long after 70 years —

I cherish kind words, these are the
propelling force to continue our journey.

And many more small events
that had huge impact on my life

Best wishes
Susan Pollack

IN RESPONSE TO YOUR LETTER ENQUIRY, here are a few thoughts that assisted me to look forward in my youth after those bleak, horrendous times in 1944. I am a camp survivor from Auschwitz and liberated in Bergen Belsen on the 15th April 1945. I was totally dehumanised, fearful, distrustful, lost to contemplate the future, all alone, unable to comprehend the values for a life in a modern civilisation.

Being brought up in a village in Hungary, removed from the sophistication of a 'new world' how can I find myself trusting others without a voice, unable to articulate any latent dislikes, that gradually emerged – that did not include me, with no one listening.

Fourteen years old – unable to walk, to express the latent, suppressed anguish – the realisation I only speak Hungarian, no skills, no education, no finance, no support system, no knowledge.

The first awareness in Bergen Belsen was the discovery that kindness and goodwill had also survived. When the British soldier lifted me up from the mud hole – seeing a twitch in my body – he gently placed me in one of the small ambulances. From that experience – miraculous goodwill is one of the guiding lights to this day. I often think of that moment and ask 'What part of that goodness with your heart you take from that soldier?'

Kindness, generosity comes in small everyday events. Small measures of goodness have an enormous impact – to this day I take nothing for granted. I remember the effect and appreciation this first helpfulness had on my life – it gradually removed the heavy iron cover on me and sparks of 'I can do' and 'want to do' gradually came into my existence.

In Sweden where I was taken for recuperation for my devastated physical corpse-like being, one of the facilitators had a large collection of classical records. These he played every evening and we sat around and listened in awe to Beethoven symphonies and other pieces. In my interpretation I could feel the energy of music from sorrow and despair to the drive of supreme human effort to rise above those destructive memories. I must say not completely – personally, I don't want to let it go completely – but I am free of the chains which deprived me in the camps. Music generally has an enormous effect on my life. I moved on. I became a Samaritan helper – 'Can I help you?' – for some 8 years.

I took a degree at the age of 60 years and then a diploma in Psychology. For me life is full of possibilities, like a search engine – find your meaning for existence that makes me feel worthy – self esteem is the reward.

I was fortunate in having a family and could play with my grandchildren, reclaiming those years of persecution.

I remember the doctor in Sweden who took me in his arms to teach me walking and turned to me saying 'I have a little girl like you.' What a discovery about myself – powerful words that still ring in my ears long after 70 years – I cherish kind words. These are the propelling force to continue our journey and many more small events that had huge impact on my life.

MARTINE WRIGHT MBE

MARTINE WRIGHT is a survivor of the 7/7 London bombings, a Paralympian and an inspirational speaker. She lost both of her legs, and 80 per cent of the blood in her body, in the Aldgate underground explosion in 2005. She was in a coma for ten days and had to undergo ten months of surgery following the injury. As part of her rehabilitation she played wheelchair tennis before focusing on sitting volleyball. In July 2012 she was selected as part of Great Britain's women's sitting volleyball team for the Summer Paralympics. After the 7/7 bombings, she campaigned for better compensation for victims of the bombings and their families, and has been an ambassador for sport for people with disabilities.

IN SOME RESPECTS, I FEEL LUCKY. That may sound strange as I was one of the victims of the atrocities of 7/7, being unlucky enough to be standing on a train too close to one of the terrorist suicide bombers who wreaked havoc in London that fateful morning. Unlike the fifty-two who lost their lives that day, I survived by the skin of my teeth after losing 80 per cent of my blood and experiencing too many operations to mention. It is ironic, because whilst I still bear the physical and mental scars of that awful experience, I have learned to live again, resetting my life and seeing things in a different perspective.

My chance at having a 'second go' at living has allowed me to not only personally fulfil many aspirations such as sky diving, learning to ski and being a celebrity *Strictly Come Dancing* contestant, but has also allowed me to share with thousands of others my experiences, my values and my tips on life through my work as an inspirational speaker. It has also helped me to deal with my history and my issues head-on, as I use my 'Power of 7' as the basis of my talk, I even wear the number 7 shirt when representing GB as a sitting volleyball athlete as a mark of respect to the fifty-two people and their surviving families.

All of that is the public side of me, but for me, meaning, purpose and fulfilment is defined by my amazing family that I have around me. My husband Nick and beautiful son Oscar are at the centre of my world, and my close and extended family who gave me hope, encouragement, reassurance and belief after my near-death experience are my reason for living. I strive each and every day to make them proud, to be the best that

I can, and to understand, as I now do, the gift of giving. So, as I say, in many respects I feel lucky. No day is taken for granted, no favour too small, and if I manage to motivate or inspire one person in a day, then I feel a tremendous sense of reward.

'I have learned to live again, resetting my life and seeing things in a different perspective.'

SIMON WESTON CBE

SIMON WESTON is a Welsh veteran of the British Army who is known for his charity work and recovery from severe burn injuries suffered during the Falklands War. In 1982, when the *RFA Sir Galahad* was destroyed in the Bluff Cove Air Attack, Weston was severely injured, sustaining serious burns to 46 per cent of his body. Following his injuries, he set up 'The Weston Spirit', a Liverpool-based young people's charity. His charitable work earned him a CBE, and led to him being awarded the Freedom of the City of London and of Liverpool. He was honoured as one of the top 100 Welsh Heroes in 2004, and in 2014 Weston was voted the UK's Favourite Hero. His story has been the subject of five major BBC Television documentaries.

WHEN I WAS SITTING on my hospital bed after my injury, aged twenty-one, I didn't know what the future held. I was at a complete loss. But I came to the conclusion that, although I didn't know what the world could offer me, all I could do was try to make the best contribution and the most positive impact possible.

People say that when a bomb goes off, if you don't get hurt by the actual wave then it sucks all the oxygen out of the air. In fact, it sucks all the oxygen out of so much of you. And so many of your loved ones, too.

When my incident happened, my initial instinct was I just had to survive. But the consequences of it led me to some very dark places with post-traumatic stress. At times, I was heavily depressed, and my love affair with alcohol became very obvious and very dependent. I was searching for happiness, although I was never going to find it in a bottle.

Fortunately I was lifted out of my pits of despair by so many people, and kindness was shown to me by soldiers, sailors, airmen and airwomen along the way. In hospital I was treated so magnificently well, and one of the things that stayed with me was the humour, and finding comedy in all situations. Acts of kindness really can be as small as making someone smile, or making them chuckle. Lots of these people probably don't even realise the impact they had, or how their actions lifted me up, but I will be forever grateful to those people who made such huge efforts to bring me comfort and to help me survive.

As I think back now to being in hospital, there was a guy called Oscar, who was a Naval Rating, onboard a little ship called the *Hydra*. I've never met Oscar since, but for three days he was so unbelievably kind to me. He wasn't a trained nurse or anything like that. He just did the best he could for me with the discomfort I was having. I've never forgotten that, and I hope that in his years afterwards he looks back at that and he feels immense pride and joy that he helped me when I was in a much darker place.

At one of my lowest points, Malcolm Brinkworth, who made the documentaries about my return to this country, arranged for me to meet Carlos, the Argentinian pilot who bombed our ship. I'd always said that I wanted to see if the pilot had life in his eyes. Carlos was approached and he was told of my nightmares and my troubles with post-traumatic stress. After being told the reason why I would like to meet him he instantly said, 'Yes, I'll meet him.' But more importantly, he straightaway qualified it and said, 'The reason I'll meet him is because I played a part in his problems. Hopefully, I can play a part in his solution.' Carlos acknowledged that I had a weakness because of what had happened. By meeting, he helped me regain the strength of my own character. He helped me understand that I could be more and, by his actions, he demonstrated what it takes to have moral courage, compassion and the desire to help. The war was over so we were no longer enemies, we were no longer on different sides of being combatants. I actually saw him again last year. I went to Argentina and spent some time with him and his family. Apart from friendship, real genuine respect has grown between us. Of course, I lost so many good friends that day of the incident, but Carlos was doing his job. And there was nothing to forgive for him doing his job, because had the roles been reversed then I would have done exactly what he did, as would every other combatant.

These interactions certainly helped me, but I'm not happy every day. I believe permanent happiness is mythical. I love Christmas, but it's like wanting Christmas Day every day for the rest of your life. It would be so boring to repeat the same things every single day. You need variety – that's why I drink both tea and coffee, and that's why I love the seasons. Joy, though, is different to happiness. We need to have more joy in our life. I get joy from art, I get joy from nature, I get joy from people, I get joy when I see a goal or a try scored.

I see life like a flat line and the aim is to stay as close to that line as possible. You could call it mundane, but that's great because you aren't suffering any severe swings of sadness, or elation. You can't live on big spikes of elation, just as you're trying to avoid great big dips below. I love the little upward blips along the way, when you're laughing, you're smiling, you're enjoying things. I try to appreciate all the little things that I do have in life, because they add up to a big thing. For example, take even reading a book – there's a joy in the fact that you can see and you can read, as there are a lot of people in the world who haven't been taught to read. There are a lot of people in the world who can't read because of dyslexia, because of blindness, and they have to read in a different way. It's not about material items. Don't get me wrong, I like having nice things, and I like having nice things for my family. But at the end of the day, as long as you're warm and you're dry and you're comfortable, that's your flat line. That's your normality. And that's what I've always worked for.

I certainly didn't ever want to be famous. It was never on my agenda, and it only came about through some terrible, tragic circumstance. I never set out for any adulation. And when it did happen, when I did become a public figure, I struggled to deal with it because I hadn't been trained for it. But now I think I'm very fortunate to have ended up in the public eye because it put me in a position to be able to go out and make a difference in other people's lives. It allowed me to take part in other people's organisations, and to set up my own in Weston Spirit.

As such, for me, the meaning of life is about being relevant. Being relevant is the hardest thing to sustain. When I finished being relevant to being in the army, I had to become relevant to something else. I had to learn to like myself, again. I'm not a great person to believe that people should love themselves. But, I do think it's important to get up in the morning, look yourself in the mirror and say, 'Yep, I like you. I genuinely like you. You're a good person, you do the best you can do with what you've got.'

I had to learn to appreciate my ability to still contribute to other people's lives, and to society. It's probably the hardest thing to continue to be relevant in people's lives. If you're not relevant to other people, you can find it very hard to be relevant to yourself. You might not be able to change the conflicts that are happening in the world, and you can't stop the poor leadership of politicians all over the globe. We can't change all of that, unless the opportunities really do present themselves. And we can't stop some of the sadnesses. But what we can do is become hugely relevant in the communities and the commitments we make and the jobs we take on.

Over the years, I've had people randomly come up to me throughout Britain, and tell me that the organisations I've been a part of have changed the direction of their lives. I believe you have to return some of what you've been given. So, so many people gave me care and love and respect and compassion and generosity, I would be the most selfish, ungrateful human if I didn't try to put something back into life. Recently, I was at a charity function and I was told about a young woman who had suffered a terrible start to her life, but thanks, in part, to Weston Spirit, she was now working as a successful backing singer for famous artists. Listening to this story meant so much to me, that I felt an enormous welling up in my chest. To play a part in people's lives like that brings me great joy. It really does. It brings me a great sense of fulfilment.

I was once told that I was totally unemployable by somebody in the military. And I just wished he could have heard that story. I wish he could have heard about all the different people that me being injured has affected positively. I realised then that I made the difference that I wanted to when I was sat on the end of my bed in the hospital, wondering what the hell I was going to do with my life.

'We need to have more joy in our life. I get joy from art, I get joy from nature, I get joy from people …'

MIKE
HAINES OBE

MIKE HAINES is best known for his campaign Global Acts of Unity. This campaign began after his brother David was brutally murdered by ISIS in Syria in 2014. In the immediate aftermath of his brother's death, Haines felt strongly that he did not want innocent Muslim people to be blamed or victimised in his name. Haines made a television appeal for unity and tolerance. Since then, he has spoken to over 100,000 people, with the aim of encouraging unity, tolerance and understanding between people from all communities. He is a board member of the NGO ACTED and one of the founder members of Survivors Against Terror.

FOR ME, THE TRUE WEALTH OF HUMANITY lies in diversity. As someone fortunate enough to travel extensively, I've had the privilege of meeting people from various cultures, faiths and creeds. These encounters are enriching – I relish learning about their backgrounds and beliefs, asking questions, and broadening my understanding.

Imagine life as a tapestry, woven from countless threads: different colours, thicknesses, materials and lengths. It's these variations that lend the tapestry its beauty and intrigue. If it were composed of a single colour, uniform thickness or identical material, it would lose its allure.

Our societies mirror this rich diversity – vibrant with life, colours, cultures, faiths and myriad differences. And these differences deserve celebration. Being Scottish doesn't make me superior to others; it's the same for everyone. No single trait elevates us above our fellow humans.

Diversity brings understanding and cooperation. It gives us different perspectives and empathy. Empathy is crucial. Exposure to diverse experiences cultivates compassion and the more differences we embrace, the stronger our connections become.

But diversity isn't solely for society – it's also personal. We should infuse diversity into our thoughts, actions and self-perception. By challenging ourselves, we grow.

In my opinion, diversity is one of life's essential elements – for ourselves, our communities and our society as a whole.

May our differences diversify us instead of dividing us.

NATALIE QUEIROZ MBE

NATALIE QUEIROZ is the founder and director of social enterprise company Inspire 2 Quit Blades, focused on reducing youth violence, preventing knife crime and empowering young people to live their best lives. She is a Domestic Abuse Survivor Ambassador, a motivational speaker and proud holder of the title MBE. In 2019, she told her story in the book *Still Standing*.

'NATALIE . . . HI, NATALIE. Do you know where you are?'

'The QE. I think I'm in the QE,' I slurred, my eyes not wanting to open properly.

'That's right, Natalie. You are in the QE. You were brought here yesterday after you were badly attacked in the street. Do you remember that?'

I nodded.

Stabbed . . . I was stabbed . . .

'You have a little baby daughter, Natalie. She is alive . . .'

What?

It's Saturday March 5th 2016 and I've just come out of my induced coma. Just twenty-four hours before my life was in its final moments of its 'happy bubble' normality, with no hint that I would be fighting for my life in the street at 3 p.m. on a Friday in a nice suburban town centre. I was eight months pregnant and fighting against a man who was in a heavy disguise. A man who proceeded to stab me twenty-four times with a twelve-inch carving knife, in a time period of nine long minutes. The man turned out to be my partner.

My world blew apart. My life never to be the same again. My view of the meaning of life to be forever changed.

Nobody could explain how I survived my injuries. Nor how my baby survived. But we both had.

In the proceeding days and weeks as my head continued to spin, one clear thought and recurring question shone through. What was actually important in my life? I had spent all my adult years striving for that next step in the career ladder, and I had been successful. Alongside having two children and a successful career in the huge corporate world of the pharmaceutical industry, I had developed my skills, gained numerous corporate successes, driven nice cars, gained financial security but had spent a LOT of time away from my family in order to be at that next managers' meeting or training course. BUT was I truly happy? Had I been true to what was actually important to me, my children? Yes I had provided them with security, but Mom was always dashing about, always packing a bag for another meeting. Had I have died that Friday afternoon in March 2016, would it really have been worth it?

During my recovery I had the bizarre and in some ways enviable position of being able to almost 'float' outside of my situation and look in, surveying all that was around me. I had to 'stop' the career drive and for the first time, I unleashed a freedom within me that I had never experienced before. I realised I had a choice.

We are all so conditioned to push on, strive for that next goal – whether that be on the corporate ladder or the housing ladder or whatever ladder we feel we need to climb. But are we actually on the right ladder? Do we always need to blindly push on up, grabbing that next rung? Or can we stop and decide to jump down and try another one? Can we dare to allow ourselves that freedom to discover what is important to us? To give ourselves that 'values' check and see if we are being true to them.

Life can make us forget those values at times. The fast-moving pace we all live at, the chaos of our family units maybe. But we have to stop and check-in on ourselves.

We all know we have one life and tragically most of us don't fully appreciate that until we nearly lose it. It took that extreme for me to have my wake-up call.

Dare to be different. Dare to try that thing. And most importantly, in my humble opinion, is to try to leave the world in a better place than how you found it. Don't make it all about you. Whether you make someone feel loved or secure, or simply bring them laughter and light, or you become a cog in a wider machine to make this world a little bit better. But always be kind. Be honest. Be true.

We never know when our last day will be, but always live with your core values at the heart of whatever you choose to do. Then, I feel, you will be living your true meaning of life.

'Had I have died that Friday afternoon in March 2016, would it really have been worth it?'

SIR TERRY WAITE

KCMG CBE

SIR TERRY WAITE is an English humanitarian, author and former Special Envoy of the Archbishop of Canterbury. It was in this role that world-wide public attention focused on Waite as he negotiated the release of several hostages from Iran, and in 1982 he negotiated with Colonel Gaddafi for the release of British hostages held in Libya. However, when negotiating for the release of Western hostages in Lebanon, in 1987, he himself was taken captive and remained a prisoner for 1,763 days, the first four years of which were spent in solitary confinement. Since his release in 1991 he has written a number of books, including the international best-seller *Taken on Trust*. He is the co-founder and president of the charity Y Care International, co-founder and chair of Hostage UK and president of Emmaus UK, the charity for the homeless.

I HAVE AN HOUR THIS AFTERNOON when I can at least attempt to give you a reply to your question.

The question you ask regarding the meaning of life is a question that has been asked since the beginning of time. Any answer given can only be a partial insight into the mystery of life itself. Life and indeed our very existence is and remains a mystery and in order to give meaning to that mystery we need to be able to develop a philosophy that will partially satisfy us and lead to a degree of fulfilment.

There is a saying that runs through my mind as I think about this question and that is 'We are co-creators with God'. By that I understand that we are responsible for this world and all that is within it. We either create or we destroy. We do not have absolute and total control of events but we do have a large measure of control. The responsibility is on the human species to make informed choices that are creative. Such an approach can give meaning to life and lead to fulfilment.

Anyone who has witnessed the death of another human being will be aware that at the time of death something will have left that body. Some would call that something the soul. Across the ages men and women have struggled to define 'soul' and it continues to be difficult to define. The human body is temporal and will die. That is beyond dispute. Some believe that the soul is spiritual and is not confined by the bounds of time. Whatever one believes if one is to find meaning and purpose in life then one would do well to take care of both body and soul. In other words to nourish our inner life as we would the body itself.

There is one key word that helps unlock the mystery and that is love. Love of our neighbour. Love of self and love of life. Where there is true love purpose, meaning and fulfilment may at least be found in part.

I hope this might be helpful James.

Yours,

Terry

'There is one key word that helps unlock the mystery and that is love.'

CHRIS
MOON MBE

CHRIS MOON is an international speaker and former British Army officer who left the army to work for a charity clearing landmines. He survived being taken prisoner in Cambodia by the Khmer Rouge, negotiating his release and that of two colleagues from threatened execution. In 1995, he was blown up in a supposedly safe area of a minefield in remote East Africa, losing his right arm and leg. He taught himself to run again and successfully completed the London Marathon and a master's degree within a year of leaving hospital. He was awarded an MBE for his work in demining, and in recognition of his humanitarian work he was given the honour of carrying the Olympic flame into the stadium at the opening ceremony of the 1998 Nagano Winter Olympics.

EVER SINCE I CAN REMEMBER I've had a fascination for the truth and understanding what's going on and why. I worked out quite quickly people's truths vary. In a relationship there is one partner's version of the truth, the other partner's version of the truth and then there's the truth. I have made much of my life about seeking the truth and pursuing wisdom, and confess sometimes to a degree of confusion.

On numerous occasions I have faced death. In a conversation with an academic who studied survival situations, I was amused to be informed I should be dead many times over. From this I worked out we should be careful who we listen to.

It took me a while to work it out, life is truly a gift we can take for granted.

In 1993, whilst working for a charity clearing landmines in Cambodia, I was taken prisoner by Khmer Rouge guerrillas. The authorities asked us to clear landmines in a village on the edge of the forest. Our security was guaranteed by three infantry battalions in the area. It was my second day operating there when we were ambushed. I was taken prisoner with two Cambodian colleagues.

When we were first hit everything happened in slow motion. I still remember it in the present tense. The thing I'll never forget about those first moments was the feeling of horror and evil and it was an external force. I was told I was a prisoner of war of the Khmer Rouge and if I didn't immediately follow the order of any soldier or if I attempted to escape, I would be immediately shot.

They knew I wasn't part of the United Nations; I wasn't wearing a soldier's uniform so they concluded I was a spy. I'd done everything I could to understand the situation in Cambodia and read everything I could get my hands on. I knew two things: there was a saying amongst KR soldiers, *It is nothing for us to kill you,* and their prisoner handling consisted of interrogation, torture and execution.

During the three days we were held, there were seven times when I thought we might be shot. When I thought I might die I asked this question: What's the point of life? What's it all about?

In those moments the meaning of life became clear. It's about finding our purpose and meaning. For each of us it will be different, and it's a journey not a destination. Perhaps it's about finding hope and keeping the faith. I most certainly have learned life is about rising above the things that drag us down.

I'd found my place in the world and I was doing something I passionately believed in; using my agricultural and military skills to protect the innocent from the debris of war which caused disability and death. If our belief and passion is for a cause greater than ourselves, the human spirit can rise above most things and in the end there will be no fear of death.

I'd felt the agony and faced the final curtain. In those moments, you think of the people you love and those who love you. I also sensed there would be a reckoning.

Every philosophy, every creed and religion has a true value for human relationships. Perhaps life is about loving and being loved and creating relationships of trust and interdependence. In the end there are some things that last for ever, for example McDonald's fries and politicians who don't like the results of the referendum who say we should keep having votes until they get the result they want – that's a neverendem. Of all the things that last for ever the greatest of these is love.

If we can do something in some small way to truly help others and make our world a better place it will add value and meaning to our own existence. We get what we give.

When it comes to meaning and purpose we need to focus on our reasons for living. It's very easy to be paralysed by what's wrong in the world, because there's so much injustice. There is also much that's good and hopeful. Perhaps standing up against what's wrong is one of the greatest purposes and meanings we can have.

I've been privileged to travel extensively around the world and have noticed that irrespective of race, creed, nationality or religion, human beings' similarities are far greater than our differences. Build bridges, lose judgement, there is little to be gained by making others wrong.

Plato said, 'The first and greatest victory is to conquer yourself; to be conquered by yourself is of all things most shameful and vile.' Here is one of our greatest challenges in life: rise above self and see the bigger picture. Darkness wins when people become the centre of their own universe.

One of the reasons I survived as a prisoner of the Khmer Rouge is because I see the bigger picture and see beyond myself. This meant I could control the fight, flight, fright response, think objectively, and analyse how to influence.

I was blown up running a large landmine clearance programme in northern Mozambique in 1995. I lost my lower right arm and leg. It's no sacrifice. I'm privileged to have done something I passionately believe in. I choose to be thankful for what I have, rather than worry about what I've lost.

So where do we find fulfilment and peace? For me the answer is making the best of our talents and being the best we can be, enjoying the journey of life, connecting with people and nature.

I did my first marathon within a year of leaving hospital having lost two limbs. I thought I was doing quite well until I got to the 11-mile point, and then I was passed by a massive gentleman wearing a huge chicken suit. In that moment I learned don't be the centre of your own universe – don't compare yourself to others, just be the best you can be. I don't want to run faster than anybody else, I just want to run faster than myself, therein is the journey to happiness, and that is why I went on to become the world's first amputee ultra distance runner.

I've been a professional speaker for many years and am frequently asked, Are you religious? My experiences have made me less religious. Man made religion; religion did not make man. I am however more spiritual. I believe there is a power of good, God, love, creativity, call it what you will. I've also experienced the opposite of that and have learned to move towards the light and be aware that sometimes the light attracts the dark. In the words of Einstein, *our technology has advanced faster than our humanity.* I hope and pray that in the future our humanity will catch up and we will preserve the beauty and creativity of nature in our world and that humanity will rise above itself.

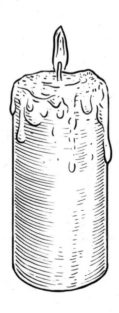

'During the three days we were held, there were seven times when I thought we might be shot. When I thought I might die I asked this question: What's the point of life? What's it all about?'

MATT LEWIS

MATT LEWIS is a shipwreck survivor. During his first deployment as a marine biologist, the fishing boat's pumps failed in the Antarctic seas, amid ocean waves the size of houses. Hundreds of miles from safety, his raft was flooded with -1°C seawater. The winter storm that sank the ship went on to claim the lives of almost half the crew, as they drifted at night. He described the sinking, and the fight for life that followed, in his best-selling book *Last Man Off*.

PERHAPS YOU WOULD EXPECT me to write that I am thankful for every day that I am alive; that each day of the twenty-five years since the ship sank has been a blessing. Surely, a shipwreck would bring some clarity to the purpose of life?

In the moments when I recall how close I came to death, then I do, indeed, remind myself how lucky I am to be here, and I am thankful for that. But my life is as chaotic and mundane and frustrating as everyone else's, and that gets in the way.

Seventeen of my crewmates died that night – ten in the same life raft as me, up to our waists in -1°C seawater. Cold-water shock and hypothermia are merciful: most of the men did not suffer, but slipped silently away. I know, because I was close behind them.

Their lives were over, but their ripples of impact were not. Each man left behind a complex web of family and friends, love and arguments, and respect and debts. Many were fathers, some of children unborn, and their offspring have now grown and set out on lives of their own. These networks that we build and leave behind allow us to survive after we have died.

A short time ago, the child of a crewmate who died contacted me. They did not appreciate the way I had described their father's actions in my book, and they wanted to defend him. I am sorry for the hurt I caused, but I could not retract or change my description – it is the best way to tell others what happened, so far from land and rescue. But the fact that the child wanted to stand up for their father shows that he still endures, albeit in their thoughts. If the meaning of life is in the impact you have, on the world or others around you, then his ripples still continue.

I find peace in telling our story to those few that may learn from it. Complacency played a massive part in the sinking of the *Sudur Havid* and there are lessons to be gained. If our story is useful to those trying to understand actions under pressure, or dealing with safety culture in industry, then it is worth telling.

I find reward in connection with other people – family, friends, readers, random encounters in another country.

I find fulfilment in movement. My mind is beautifully focused and untroubled when I am outdoors, flowing along a trail or across water.

For me, the damage was not caused by the shard of ice in my cells, but from watching other men suffer and being too weak to help.

But, then, that also means that:

The beauty and the healing in life is to reach out, talk with, touch and offer a hand to those around you.

Matt

'Surely, a shipwreck would bring some clarity to the purpose of life?'

BRIAN CLARK

BRIAN CLARK is a Canadian businessman and survivor of the attacks on the World Trade Center on 11 September 2001. Clark worked for the American international brokerage firm Euro Brokers Inc., which lost sixty-one employees that day, nearly one-fifth of its New York branch. Clark was one of only eighteen people in the South Tower to escape from within or above the impact zone where the plane struck, escaping from his office on Floor 84. Clark was later appointed by his company's management to be president of the Euro Brokers Relief Fund, created to help take financial care of the families of those who were lost.

I WAS FORTUNATE TO HAVE SURVIVED a difficult situation at New York's World Trade Center on September 11, 2001.

Life has found new meaning for me after that experience. Here are some snippets that I have come to realize . . .

THINGS IN THE PAST

I can ask myself, 'Why did I survive? Why not others?'

But logically those are two unanswerable questions.

I now know that it is a waste of time to worry about unanswerable questions or even try to answer them because they are, in fact, unanswerable.

I now suggest that if anyone is encountering such 'unanswerable' questions that they do not waste energy on such imponderable things that have happened in the past.

THE FUTURE

Focus more on the future. Doing so moves you forward and away from the thing that is troubling you. In most cases when you are stuck, that's a good thing.

At the same time, don't worry about the future . . . Because you cannot say with any certainty what the future is going to be, or how it's going to unfold.

It's great to have plans but you have no idea if those plans will come to fruition as you expect. Don't worry about it. Things will unfold and you'll adjust. We humans are quite amazing in that regard.

THE PRESENT

If you don't dwell on 'unanswerables' from the past, and you don't worry about the future, it leaves you with the present. That's where I live now . . . Very much in the present.

With a smile on my face, I tell people, 'Every day is a great day; some are just greater than others.'

And following my escape on 9/11, I have good reason to tell young people, 'Life is very precious.'

MOVING FORWARD

I now encourage myself and others to be useful, and to 'live well' with all the time we have left.

By that, I mean we should all strive to use our gifts and talents to better our own lives and also to better the lives of those around us . . . our families, our neighbors, our towns and cities, our nations, our world. Such work will bring you happiness.

I want people to 'love well'. Have you told the people whom you love that you do indeed love them? I know they want to hear it. And I know you want to hear that you are loved by them.

When our individual lives come to an end, if you can look back and know that you have 'lived well' and that you have 'loved well', your legacy will be that the world is in a better place for you having been there.

'I have good
reason to tell
young people,
"Life is very
precious."'

JOHN HOSKISON

JOHN HOSKISON is a former professional golfer who competed on the European Tour alongside the likes of Sir Nick Faldo, Seve Ballesteros and Ian Woosnam. In 1994, however, he broke a discipline he had maintained for twenty years and accepted a drink after a golf match before driving home. On his short journey he hit and killed a cyclist and was sentenced to three years in prison. For the last fifteen years, Hoskison has tried to make up for what happened. He has spoken at over 200 schools, to over 80,000 children, about the dangers of taking unnecessary risks. He has also attended many conferences about how to improve prison and has spoken to many of the top judges in the country, regularly attending the Judicial Studies Board Seminars. After many years in the darkness, in 2007, with the blessing of everyone concerned, he took his European Seniors Tour Card and finished 2nd to gain full playing privileges.

AT A YOUNG AGE I BECAME a professional sportsman. At just seventeen I was a trainee professional golfer at the RAC Country Club in Epsom and within three years of that I was on the European Tour. Vertical trajectory. I was trained to see life in black and white. Success or failure. Good and bad. I thought of little else but my career. I mixed with some of the most successful businessmen in the country and some of the best athletes in the world.

I wasn't particularly happy though. I'd had a lousy time at boarding school when I was eleven. My parents insisted on me taking A-levels in one year at fifteen. After a family row at sixteen, I ran away from home. Weird times.

But at the RAC I had recovered and flourished. It was tough work. My hands bled from hitting golf balls. I'd lie awake every night trying to find a way to get better. Incredibly, ten years later, I went on to play for England in the European Team Championships and twice I represented Europe against America in PGA Cup matches. My dream had come true. I had everything a man could wish for. Strangely enough the material wealth I gained didn't mean much to me and I gave away most of what I didn't need.

Playing the European Tour meant spending many hours travelling on my own. Lots of time to think and I started to realise I led a very limited life. I invested my time investigating different philosophies and was particularly attracted to the concept of giving up the eternal struggle to reach the summit and instead turn round on the mountain and survey the view. That opened my eyes and for the first time I started to realise that many of the magnificent golf courses I visited were often surrounded by areas of poverty and squalor.

Then one day I made a terrible mistake and my life changed for ever. I took the risk of drinking and driving and I caused a fatal accident.

Inevitably it led to a prison sentence. But I received a gift from a remarkable woman. My expected five years behind bars was brought down to three by the incredible forgiveness shown to me by the widow who pleaded for leniency to be shown at my sentencing trial.

But a prison sentence loomed ahead of me. In the year it took for my sentencing trial to get to court I tried to picture what prison would be like. The reality was totally different to anything I had imagined. Not just in the feeling of claustrophobia locked away in a small cell but also in the people I lived with. They were no longer world-class athletes at the breakfast table contemplating their next international flight. More often than not I was surrounded by haunted men, hooked on heroin, consumed with where to get their next fix.

Before going to prison I would have dismissed my fellow inmates as bad people. What happened to them was deserved. But as I spent months getting to know them, I came to understand that life is not that simple.

Having been forgiven for my crime, I was in a position where I tried to understand how people got into trouble. My early life had been so privileged. Private school, sporting facilities, doctors . . . But what if I'd been brought up in the squalor and deprivation my fellow inmates had experienced. Gang life would have been inevitable. My competitive gene would have probably driven me to climb to the top by pushing more drugs than anyone else. I couldn't help feel that society had let down many of the young men I met.

Somehow I survived my time inside. I avoided getting weaned onto drugs and beaten to pulp. When the riots kicked off, inmates I had met actively protected me from harm and I owe them a massive debt. When the gates finally opened I literally sank to my knees in thanks.

Incredibly the PGA invited me back into the professional ranks.

People were so kind to me and over the years, with my confidence growing, I started to give talks to young people to help them avoid trouble.

I've now delivered over 800 and I like to feel it's helped. In the early years of giving talks I was getting closer to understanding the meaning of my life.

I finally understood it when in 2019 my wife and I downsized, de-cluttered and took the plunge of moving into a park home site in Hampshire. About sixty-five glorified caravans erected on bricks. The first morning a resident of the park walked towards our home clearly intending to greet us. I went out to talk to him and in that precise moment the pieces fell into place and I found the meaning to my life.

We have become part of a caring community. Everyone looks after each other. No one faces a problem alone. I had lived life fundamentally on my own but suddenly I became part of a big team where people are genuinely concerned about your welfare. The meaning of my life became very clear. True happiness comes from giving back more than you take. By helping other people survive the pitfalls of life with support both mental and physical. Living in a caring community, wanting to invest in the welfare of others and seeing the difference kindness can make has become my ultimate reward.

BENEDICT ALLEN

TOM TURCICH

ANN DANIELS

DAME ELLEN MacARTHUR

MARK BEAUMONT BEM

BEN SMITH

YVES ROSSY

JESSICA WATSON

FATIMA WHITBREAD MBE

CHRIS EUBANK

GAIL MULLER

SIR RANULPH FIENNES

BONITA NORRIS

ALEXANDER CAMPBELL

DAVID SMITH MBE

Athletes & Adventurers

BENEDICT ALLEN

BENEDICT ALLEN is one of the world's leading modern-day explorers, through expeditions famously achieved without phone, GPS or 'backup'. While initially known mostly for his technique of immersing himself among indigenous peoples, Allen went on to establish the adventure genre in television, through his self-filmed BBC series. His many expeditions include a first recorded crossing of the Amazon Basin at its widest, and the first known traverse of the entire Namib on foot. His journeys are depicted in his ten books – including two *Sunday Times* best-sellers – and six BBC television series.

AS IT HAPPENS, I'm just organising myself to disappear into West Papua, so am rather pressed. But I'll give it a go, in a few heartfelt words. The below I'll bash out, off the top of my head. Hope it works for you!

To be honest, as a child I didn't seem to be able to make much sense of the world. Although I did join in with everyone – play football and so on – I seemed to need to work harder to find joy and satisfaction in the world around me. And, as someone who buried himself in books, this contributed to my feeling that I was meant to be some sort of explorer, like Livingstone or Scott of the Antarctic. The answer to life must be out there somewhere in the far-off forests, plains and deserts of the world. It was a question of going out and searching for it.

And off I went. And I did find fulfilment, and I did find meaning. But it was never easy – and even to this day, aged sixty-three, I don't find it easy to be satisfied.

However, I did learn that being unsatisfied 'goes with the territory'. All explorers are like this – they are searchers who are determined to find the truth that surely lies out there somewhere. Even if it in fact doesn't! But we head out there anyway, despite the risks, despite the physical discomfort. And somehow or other we come back, and feel better for it. We have scratched the itch, as it were.

But here's the thing: ALL of us in the end are explorers. This restlessness, this questing spirit, is part of what makes us human. And there's solace to be found in that: we are all in it together. And the important thing is to accept that being a human isn't easy – just as it isn't easy undergoing one of my journeys. Terrible things can happen along the way. Personally, I'm someone who has contracted malaria six times. I've been shot at, I've been robbed and left to die. But I still keep going because in the end the rewards in life are so great. The lows are low, but the highs are out of this world.

So I keep striding onward, and I thank my lucky stars that I have been allowed to live to see so much of our beautiful world.

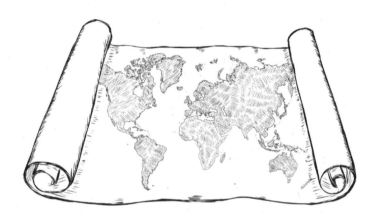

'I've been shot at,
I've been robbed
and left to die. But
I still keep going
because in the end
the rewards in life
are so great.'

TOM TURCICH

TOM TURCICH is an adventurer who circumnavigated the globe on foot. After the death of his friend, Turcich reconsidered what he wanted out of the brief time we have here. He decided to walk. By travelling slowly, he knew he would be immersed in unknown places, forced into adventure, and come to better understand the world. He started his journey in 2015, and along the way was held up at knifepoint in Panama and gunpoint in Turkey, wandered deep within himself in the deserts of Peru, and watched a democracy fortify itself in Georgia. Seven years and 28,000 miles later, Turcich and his dog, Savannah, became the tenth person and first dog to walk around the world.

CONSIDER WHO AMONG US you have to answer this question – men and women at the height of developed countries, blessed with space enough to philosophize free from the fickle whims of war, famine, and disease. Of course, every person's perspective is valid. Each of us resides in a universe of equal complexity and depth, but it's presumptuous to pass down meaning to any common denominator.

What of the worker harvesting sugar cane in El Salvador? What of the rancher guiding their cattle over the Sahel? What of the girls who have been stolen, mutilated, and dragged through history? Will you speak to them of free will? Will you speak to them of drive, motivation, and want-to?

We are smaller than we realize (or would care to admit). We are grains of salt dissolving in a vast sea of unknowable reach. To presume meaning is as arrogant as it is foolish; the illusion of self-importance is the greatest destroyer of our world. Citizens caught in their own narrow perspective become incapable of compromise or compassion. With power, self-assured, unchecked meaning results in the same ideologues responsible for our most horrific atrocities.

The only lasting measure of a man's worth is the happiness he possesses and the happiness he creates. Every other manmade construct in this world, even meaning, is in pursuit of that end. We want a home and a loving partner for security, we desire fame and accolades because of the respect they imbue, and we strive to achieve our dreams in the belief that we might ascend our humanity and unlock a state of perpetual self-acceptance. Yet the winding paths to security, respect, and self-acceptance are merely differing routes in pursuit of the same grail – happiness.

For those of us fortunate enough to reside in places with sufficient security and wealth to feign self-direction, being happy and creating happiness is a worthy aim. In most ways, the pursuit of happiness is best achieved by embracing your humanity. This means avoiding the industrialized pressure to hew yourself to an automaton of efficiency. Exercise, sleep well, surround yourself with nature, and spend time with your family. Accept that you will have bad days and forgive yourself. When others have a bad day, forgive them as well. Have a small purpose too; it need not be something as lofty and amorphous as a meaning to life, a passion to give structure to your days will do.

But even these are luxuries. If you are being crushed by the infinite forces more enormous than a single human life, it is enough to simply observe.

Do your best to lean into yourself and retain the thought, 'So this is life? I shouldn't know any better, it's my first time here.' This isn't the meaning of life, there is no meaning to life, but that's okay. You're alive. The world is abounding with beautiful complexity and filled with kind, interesting and engaging people. Do away with self-importance. Pay attention. That's enough.

'To presume
meaning is as
arrogant as it
is foolish; the
illusion of self-
importance is the
greatest destroyer
of our world.'

ANN DANIELS

ANN DANIELS is a record-breaking polar explorer and the first woman in history, along with expedition teammate Caroline Hamilton, to reach the North and South Poles as part of all-women teams. With no previous outdoor experience and as a mother of toddler triplets, she beat off fierce competition from over 200 other women to join the first team of the McVitie's Penguin Polar Relay – a unique relay expedition of women sledge hauling to the North Pole. This unique expedition was the start of a number of world-record-breaking expeditions, and she has since sledge hauled for over 400 days and 3,000 miles on the ice. Daniels has also worked with NASA, the European Space Agency and many scientific institutions globally, tracking and measuring ice and collecting data at the extreme ends of the planet, to help understand the environmental impact humans are having on the world.

FOR ME, THE MEANING OF LIFE changes as age and life's circumstances change but possibly the one thing that has remained constant for me is the desire to do better, to be more.

I thought it was right that I opened up personally for this study rather than talk about the things I am known for. If I want to be more and do better then what better place to start than at the beginning and with the real me.

I was brought up with four older brothers and when I was younger I was always the first to take on the dares, to climb the derelict building, jump the ridiculously large river, or stand in front of a tree while a brother's friend tried to hit an apple on top of my head, with a dart. Usually with the end result of a cut head, a bloody knee or in the case of the tree incident, being carried home with a dart stuck in my forehead. I was always afraid before taking on the challenge but the fear didn't deter me or stop my enthusiasm for the next ridiculous challenge or dare thrown out by my older siblings. It was almost certainly coming from the position of wanting to be one of the boys or so my brothers would let me come along with them and think I was big and brave even though I was tiny in stature. It was childish and simple but in hindsight it gave me purpose and made me attempt things I wouldn't otherwise do.

As I grew older and got my first real job, which was in a bank, a first for my family, I also wanted to progress as much as possible and worked hard to improve and do well. If I look back, my motivation was once again emotional. I wanted to prove myself, so that my more experienced peers would respect me and think I was hard working and good at my job. I don't ever recall having a desire to be a bank manager or thinking it was a fantastic job in its own right. My motivation came from another place.

A change came in me with the birth of my first children or rather the pregnancy. Having three children growing inside of me was both terrifying and wonderful and I immediately felt protective towards them. I know I was lucky and it doesn't happen to every woman but for me it was instantaneous. I was told it would be terribly difficult having three new babies and I wouldn't cope but I was sure I would prove everyone wrong and not because I cared what they thought about me, because I didn't, but because I had three lives that were more important than my own. I was used to striving and taking on challenges by then and when they were born, just four weeks early, taking care of those innocent and helpless human beings became my purpose and my focus. Sure it was tough and life was manic. I lost the 6 stone extra pregnancy weight in three weeks of new motherhood but I was riding high on adrenalin and happiness. In my mind I was completely fulfilled.

That feeling came crashing down with the demise of my marriage, which began to fall apart not long after the babies were born. I had taken my eye off the ball and didn't spot it immediately and when it finally dawned on me, it was too late. At first I began to drown in sorrow and helplessness and yes a feeling of worthlessness. Whilst I still did everything physically for my children, emotionally I wasn't coping. The meaning of life and fulfilment was a black void.

Like so many things good and bad, there's often a pivotal moment that leads to a decision to do something. For me it was a panic attack whilst playing with my eighteen-month-old babies in the dining room and seeing the fear in their eyes, as their mother struggled to breathe. I had to do something. It was now up to me, not to just take care of my beautiful children physically but emotionally as well and as a whole person, not a fearful, unworthy and terrified shell of a person, which is how I was feeling. I didn't know what that something would be but it came in the most unlikely form.

I was told of an advert asking for ordinary women to apply to be part of the first all-female team to walk/ski to the North Pole. As a mother of triplets who had never been skiing and without any outdoor experience whatsoever, there was every reason I should not apply or go on the selection weekend and whilst I was afraid, my childhood experiences and the ability to harness fear and do it anyway came in.

I applied and was hopeless for the first selection weekend but as the team was being selected on a second selection nine months later the opportunity was still there for the taking. It was an opportunity for me personally and for us as a whole. I caught a dream for the first time in my life. This could change our lives. I had purpose, vision and a goal. Life began to have a spark of meaning again.

For the next nine months I channelled everything into looking after three small children and getting onto this team. If I wasn't feeding or dressing the kids, I was training or learning map reading and the skills needed to operate in the great outdoors. Once again life was manic but it didn't feel hard or awful. I had purpose, meaning and a worthy goal. It wasn't just about the North Pole, it was my own personal goal to survive and be a full, proper human being again. To be able to look after my children on more than a basic level and to find my smile again.

Nine months later I returned to Dartmoor, where both selection weekends took place and after a gruelling four days I got on the team. I couldn't believe it and I truly believe that is my greatest achievement in my expedition career. Bigger than any of the world records, the scientific expeditions even. Only I know what it took to get there and it's where I found myself and who I wanted to be. I went home feeling worthy, able and happy and in my opinion that's a good place to be.

The rest of my expedition achievements have been well documented but here goes:

The first expedition was a relay of five teams of four women with two female guides hauling sledges to the North Pole. On that expedition I was on the first leg and didn't get to the pole on that occasion.

From these humble beginnings, myself and four other women skied from the edge of Antarctica to the South Pole and in 2002, as part of another all-female team, with Pom Oliver and Caroline Hamilton became the first and at the time of writing, the only women in history to ski to the North and South Poles as part of all-women teams.

Achieving these goals fulfilled my life and gave it purpose and meaning but eventually that wasn't enough to be meaningful for me. By then, my speaking career had taken off and I was financially stable. Not rich but then that had never been one of my goals. I had lost the desire to live life on the edge of existence, in extreme expeditions with no other purpose than to get there.

If I was going to go through that kind of physical hardship, it had to mean something more. I had grown to love the icy ends of the world and my experiences up there gave me the knowledge of what was happening to the fragile ends of our planet. The world and I were at last waking up to the devastating impacts of climate change throughout the whole planet.

My old friend and amazing expedition leader Pen Hadow was also looking to add real value to his expeditions and he put together the high-profile Catlin Arctic surveys. The only aim of these expeditions was to work with scientists to help understand what is happening in the high arctic and the effect it has throughout the world. He asked me to join him by navigating and path finding at the front of the team, so he could concentrate on the scientific aspects of the expedition. Once again I found real purpose and meaning in my career and worked with the ice team for three expeditions over three years.

I have since worked with NASA, The European Space Agency and many scientific institutions on various expeditions, tracking and measuring ice and collecting data at the extreme ends of the planet, in the hope of helping real scientists understand the environmental impact humans are having on the world.

The meaning of life has now changed dramatically for me. I was lucky enough to marry again and have four grown-up children. I am older and my children are independent and I am at my happiest if I can serve and be of help. There have been no North Pole expeditions since 2018 and I now find meaning and fulfilment helping teams in both the business world and as a climate change ambassador. I have purpose and feel of value. Who knows what will come next but as I barrel towards sixty I am content and happy.

'The meaning of life has now changed dramatically for me.'

Dame ELLEN MacARTHUR

DAME ELLEN MacARTHUR made yachting history in 2005, when she became the fastest solo sailor to circumnavigate the globe and she remains the UK's most successful offshore racer ever. Having become acutely aware of the finite nature of the resources on which our linear economy relies, she retired from professional sailing to launch the Ellen MacArthur Foundation in 2010. The Foundation works to accelerate the transition to a circular economy and has helped establish the subject on the agenda of decision-makers around the world.

I HAVE ALWAYS APPROACHED LIFE looking for a goal – whatever that may be – which helps orientate decisions and direction. This provides meaning for my life.

I also enter into all I do by saying I'll do my best. Whether it's a race or trying to shift the global economy from linear to circular.

Finally, I always try to be kind and treat people as I would like to be treated myself, and have fun in all I do.

MARK
BEAUMONT BEM

MARK BEAUMONT is a British long-distance cyclist, broadcaster and author. Among other Guinness World Records he remains the fastest person to have cycled around the planet, completing his 18,000-mile (29,000 km) route on 18 September 2017, having taken less than seventy-nine days. He has also cycled from Anchorage, Alaska, to Ushuaia in Southern Argentina; joined a six-man team to row from Resolute Bay in the Nunavut Territory, Canada, to the 1996 location of the North Magnetic Pole; and cycled from Cairo to Cape Town, breaking the world record for fastest solo ride for the length of Africa by finishing in forty-two days and eight hours.

THE MEANING OF LIFE IS about finding happiness, which I have found is a long way from contentment. Contentment suggests a static state, whereas I have always found greatest happiness in striving for something – in journeys. And my definition of success has changed hugely as I have grown older and my views on the world have changed. I am lucky in that I have been able to travel so widely, which has constantly helped me question my opinions and to reassess what is important.

The single most important event in my life for figuring out what my real priorities should be was capsizing and nearly drowning mid Atlantic. It was only by living through this and really experiencing the fragility of my own mortality that I figured out what was most important: my family.

You travel the world over in order to come home and appreciate what you have. Religion does not have a place in my own life, but I am fascinated by cultures and their history.

The meaning of life is brilliantly simple: it's about making time to create memories.

In this way we get greater pleasure as we grow older from giving than receiving and from looking after rather than being looked after.

BEN SMITH

BEN SMITH is a marathon runner who completed a record-breaking 401 marathons in 401 days. During his 10,506.2-mile odyssey criss-crossing the UK, he ran in 309 different locations, accompanied by more than 13,500 people. Smith visited 101 schools, burned an estimated 2.4 million calories and braved every extreme of the British weather, while raising £330,000 for charities Kidscape and Stonewall. In 2016, he received the Helen Rollason Award at the BBC Sports Personality of the Year Awards. Smith wrote the book *401: The Extraordinary Story of the Man Who Ran 401 Marathons in 401 Days and Changed His Life Forever* about his struggles with mental health, bullying and divorce. He launched the 401 Foundation to provide grants to organisations and individuals to focus on self-esteem and mental health.

I BELIEVE WE HAVE ONE physical life on this Earth, and that is finite. But I think we live multiple lives within our lifetime.

Before my 401 Challenge, I'd spent much of my life being driven by what other people wanted me to do. I'd been shaped by experiences that I went through at school, especially by internalised homophobia. And then, aged twenty-nine, I suffered a TIA – a transient ischaemic attack – where I suddenly realised the fragility of life.

It was almost like something clicked inside me. But it wasn't like I suddenly had all the answers, or not in the way that the movies want you to believe. In fact, I initially felt more lost. I knew I needed to change, I knew I needed things to work differently, but I had no idea how to do that.

For so many years, I didn't believe that I could live life as a gay man, I didn't believe that I could be happy. So it was important for me to come to terms with who I am as a person, accepting that, and being proud of that.

Doing this gave me a sense of power – that I could take all the energy that I'd spent using over the years, covering up who I was, and reinvesting that into something else. So that's how the challenge came about.

Running 401 marathons in 401 days was not about proving anything to anybody. It was because I wanted to raise money for Kidscape and Stonewall, two anti-bullying charities.

During the course of the challenge, I was joined by 13,500 people running with me on different days. The whole ethos of the project was about getting people on board, because to spread awareness, make a change and raise the money we needed to raise, I couldn't be the only voice shouting.

I loved every single day of the amazing challenge. But, of course, there were moments of loneliness, there were moments of elation, there were moments of sadness, there were moments of frustration, and, when I finished, there were moments of depression.

I'd been on this journey of finding myself, culminating in this challenge, and then suddenly it ended. Not only had nobody ever run 401 marathons in 401 days before, meaning there were no medical journals to read through and know what the impact was, but suddenly there was a different type of pressure.

From that moment to this day, the first question many people ask me is 'So what's next?'

It's ironic, given I'd said to myself I'd never be governed again by what other people wanted me to be but here I was in that position again. I never went into running with the intent to do big global challenges, but there was suddenly an expectation to do something else.

I was conflicted as I knew I needed to take a step back and consolidate. But my brain was thinking, I need to do something bigger. Something better. I wanted to raise more money for the 401 Foundation, so we went ahead, and we planned to do the big America Challenge (to run and cycle 10,700 miles across the USA in eighty-eight days).

Then the pandemic hit, and over the course of the following three years, due to the various restrictions, we lost the team, and the funding which we'd had in place. We'd put so much effort in, and everything was tied to our fundraising goals, that it felt like we had to go anyway. So I ended up going on my own. It was a very different challenge to what it should have been, and it didn't work. I came back to the UK with my tail between my legs, and I had the feeling of having unfinished business, which is not somewhere I wanted to be.

To be honest with you, I don't enjoy running any more. I made a conscious decision last year to take a year off running, and that was because I was finding that running wasn't bringing me any happiness, it wasn't bringing me joy. In fact, it was actually adding stress to my life. I don't know whether or not I'll go back to running, or whether I'll find joy in it again.

I've realised, though, that physical challenges aren't the only way for us to achieve our fundraising goals. I can achieve what I want to achieve in different ways. I'm definitely more content now, and I think I've returned to my pre-challenge mindset of not being driven by what other people want from me anymore.

Our Foundation strap-line is 'find your happy'. I think it's important for us to all find what makes us happy in life. But equally, as cheesy as it sounds, I'm a firm believer in the fact that happiness isn't a destination. It's not a final point. Happiness is the process, it's the journey. It's about finding happiness in the things that we do and the people that we meet. Happiness isn't a constant thing, and it's important to learn this, because if you're constantly trying to be happy that's hugely unrealistic.

Likewise, the meaning of life is not something that you find, and then everything is okay for the rest of your life. Things come and go. I think it's about being content with the fact there will be change throughout life, and about having the skills and ability to change with that. We will have multiple purposes in our lives. As long as for me, those purposes are driven by my own internal compass then I'm on the right track. The moment they're determined by other people's views, then I think that's when we start getting lost.

Over the last five years, I've had the privilege of talking to over 280,000 people in all five continents of the world, from massive global businesses to tiny primary schools. I stand up and talk very openly about my story, and maybe I was put onto the planet to show vulnerability can be a strength.

The 401 Foundation is about building a brighter, more compassionate future for people suffering with mental health. It's about being able to provide people with the right support that they need in the right way at the right time. Because we're all different. We all suffer in different ways at different times. And we require different things. That is what we're trying to do, and it's going to take some work. If anything, you could argue that's probably my next challenge.

YVES ROSSY

YVES ROSSY, also known as 'Jetman', is a pilot, adventurer and inventor. He is the first and only man in the history of aviation to fly with a jet-propelled wing. Using his invention, he has made dramatic flights over the English Channel, the Grand Canyon, Rio de Janeiro and around Mount Fuji. Rossy has developed and built a system comprising a back pack with semi-rigid aeroplane-type carbon-fibre wings, and is able to propel himself through the sky at upwards of 190mph, controlling his jet suit with a throttle in his hand, climbing over 4,000 metres and travelling as far as 16 kilometres.

I FEEL VERY LUCKY that you asked my opinion on this matter. I like the simplicity, even if the answer to this question could be developed in a much longer and deeper way, depending on the physical state in which you find yourself to answer it, especially not being hungry or thirsty . . . I'm not sure you'll find many respondents in a refugee camp who have only one priority, to survive until the next day.

That said, here's my answer to your question:

'Learn and have fun following your imagination, reducing constraints to a minimum, to share your life and experiences with those you love.'

Best regards and Blue Sky!

Yves 'Jetman' Rossy

JESSICA WATSON

JESSICA WATSON became the youngest person to sail solo nonstop around the world, aged sixteen, navigating some of the world's most remote oceans, surviving seven knockdowns and 210 days alone at sea. On completion of the voyage, Watson was met by the then Australian Prime Minister, Kevin Rudd, who declared her a national hero.

THANKS FOR THINKING OF ME in relation to your study of 'life's meaning'.

There are so very many wonderful things and simple pleasures that give my life meaning. Strong relationships with friends and family and connections with great people are among the most important to me.

But perhaps the two things that give me the most meaning are: the incredible sense of achievement that can only be gained through hard work, and the ability to make a positive impact, great or small.

I hope this short response will meet your needs, I currently feel a little young to give the subject too much reflection.

Thanks,

Jessica

March 2018

FATIMA
WHITBREAD MBE

FATIMA WHITBREAD is a retired British javelin thrower. After being abandoned by her mother as a baby, Whitbread spent her first fourteen years in a variety of care homes. She took up the javelin at the age of eleven and was chosen for the Moscow Olympics while still a teenager. She won the gold medal at the 1987 World Championships, bronze at the 1984 Summer Olympics and silver at the 1988 Summer Olympics. She won the same medals, respectively, in the Commonwealth Games of 1982 and 1986. Whitbread was voted BBC Sports Personality of the Year in 1987, and in 2023 she received the Helen Rollason Award in recognition of her triumph over the adversity of her childhood, and her continued work on behalf of other children in care environments.

IF YOU ADD VALUE TO other people's lives, you'll never be at a loss for living a life of purpose. The purpose is what ultimately leads to happiness.

Society emphasizes success a great deal, and some people overreact to it by being overly harsh on themselves, on their perceptions of what success is.

Rather, ask yourself, how can I add value today? And then do it.

My learning is that you're going to fail. If you do anything at all in life that is noteworthy. On the other hand, if you play it safe you might not fail. But then you probably didn't reach your fullest potential, either.

Failure is fine. It's how you respond to it that makes all the difference in the world.

Don't blame anyone for the failure, least of all yourself. Simply acknowledge what has happened, note what you've learned and how you'd do it differently next time, and move on.

Make no excuses.

They are simply a waste of everybody's time. Worst comes to worst, you've learned something new that makes you a more multi-dimensional person, an interesting person. After all, it's not failing that matters, but learning from our failures.

And if you don't try, how can you possibly fail in the first place?

CHRIS EUBANK

CHRIS EUBANK is a British former professional boxer who competed from 1985 to 1998. He held the World Boxing Organization middleweight and super-middleweight titles between 1990 and 1995, and is ranked by BoxRec as the third best British super-middleweight boxer of all time. He reigned as world champion for over five years, was undefeated in his first ten years as a professional, and remained undefeated at middleweight. His world title contests against fellow Britons Nigel Benn and Michael Watson helped British boxing ride a peak of popularity in the 1990s.

THE QUESTION, 'the meaning of life' is the premise by which society has misled the masses as one cannot find out the meaning of life until one simply understands that life is a gift.

When one understands that life is a gift, only then can one purposely start using their own cosmic mind (imagination that is creativity) to manifest whatever eventuality one desires.

Simply

Cx

GAIL MULLER

GAIL MULLER is an adventurer, educator and best-selling author. However, she wasn't always able to adventure, being told in her teens she'd likely lose the ability to walk by the age of forty. Muller was not deterred, and although she had to overcome over fifteen years of chronic illness she never gave up hope, and recovered to take her first steps towards a new and fulfilled life. After searching the world for a diagnosis, she was finally able to rehab her body, and in 2019 she took the body she nearly lost to hike the Appalachian Trail – almost 2,200 miles of wilderness, mountains and remote terrain. She even completed the last 850 miles with two broken bones in her foot.

MEANING IS AN INTERESTING WORD; a movable feast. I often know more about what I might mean in service of *others* than I know what my own life means to me. I think I feel most purposeful and at my happiest when I can see the effect of my touch on the world in the lifting of others. If I live for myself alone, and seek purpose *only* for myself, then I feel I live in melancholy isolation. It's often only when plunging myself into the energies that connect us all, and trying to add more than I take, that meaning courses through me.

My grandfather once told me that it's impossible to build true happiness on the unhappiness of others; that those foundations will not be strong or good. At a young age, I took this to mean that even if such a structure seems to thrive, it creaks and sighs internally with some sort of knowing about where its feet lie; a subsidence of the soul, so to speak. I've always taken this to heart as a core tenet. I think I've found my most contentment in life when helping others to create happy foundations for themselves, on good ground, so that they can build true, strong structures in their lives. I have certainly seen this succeed in my years of working with my students in schools, and now in my work as a coach and speaker; helping others to see that their foundations are strong, or in supporting them to make them so. I'm not idealistic enough to think this can always happen, but I do believe that there's meaning in trying to find the way of least harm when moving through this world, even if it's not always entirely achievable. We are all only here for a short while, so why not try to contribute to the future world being good in some way, rather than only focusing on what we feel we need here and now, today.

Building happiness on good foundations not only applies to individuals, I strongly believe that it also applies to how we work with, and on, our planet. The Earth gives us huge amounts of advice on how to live a meaningful life, even if 'happiness' isn't really on her agenda of considerations. Happiness comes with feeling aligned, and nature is always trying to align itself. The balance of seasons, rest and play, the way the natural world supports itself in thriving symbiotic relationships; knowing and understanding these things give us mental medicine for seeking balance and alignment in our own lives. How much we take and how much we give matters. I know that when I'm out of sync on the 'give and take' seesaw, that my life feels much less meaningful or happy.

I chose not to have children, and am single; both things which put me in a place where some of the key traditionally understood 'purposes' and 'meanings' are missing from my life. But I don't feel that not having these makes me have less meaning. In fact, it helps me to look for purpose *beyond* myself and my own need to keep a family thriving; it gives me freedom to think more about what I'm for, if I wasn't meant for being a mother (in the biological sense). I won't lie, there are times that I feel quite sad and lost without this obvious purpose and wonder whether, as animals, procreation *is* what gives us meaning, but then I see litter to pick up, friends to support, have ideas to write for my next book, trails to hike and people who might need some time, energy and a mirror to shine their light back to them so they can see all their inner and outer beauty more clearly. It's then that I know exactly what the meaning of my life is; to get my hands in the earth in the service of others, and to help them make good happy ground for the foundations of their purposeful and meaningful lives too.

I haven't always made the right decisions, and I haven't always been 'good', but in my late thirties and now in my forties I have definitely woken up to the things I thought I wanted but that actually weren't right; what felt meaningless to me and what made me feel good. I've never followed a traditional pathway in any sense, and with ADHD I've often pinballed through wild, dangerous and seemingly senseless trajectories which have done me more harm than good, but these experiences of being pushed all over the map, both literally and internally, have given me a wider view of what real happiness and meaning feels and looks like. I've worked with the unhappiest billionaires, and with most centred, radiantly happy folks who had next to nothing in the material sense. Across all this terrain of life I could clearly see that the further you get away from balance in what you give and what you take out of this life, the less contentment and happiness you feel. So I use my skills to help others find their purpose and balance too, and seeing others thrive from those strong foundations gives my life meaning.

Sending my very best to you, and thank you for giving me cause and pause to think over this wonderful question.

Gail

Sir RANULPH FIENNES

SIR RANULPH FIENNES is a British explorer, writer and poet. He was the first person to visit both the North Pole and the South Pole by surface means, and the first to completely cross Antarctica on foot. In 2009, at the age of sixty-five, he climbed to the summit of Mount Everest.

27 Oct 2015

Dear James Bailey,

Thanks for yours –

I'm totally non-introspective &
non-philosophical –

The only internal thoughts &
general 'wonderings' I've had
are in my autobiography book
obtainable via Kindle or
Amazon or e-bay.
Title 'Mad Bad & Dangerous to Know'

Hope it helps.

Best wishes

Ran Fiennes

THANKS FOR YOURS.

I'm totally non-introspective and non-philosophical.

The only internal thoughts and general 'wonderings' I've had are in my autobiography book obtainable via Kindle or Amazon or eBay.

Title 'Mad Bad & Dangerous to Know.'

Hope it helps.

Best wishes,

Ran Fiennes

BONITA NORRIS

BONITA NORRIS is a world-renowned adventurer, who, aged twenty-two, became the youngest woman at the time to summit Mount Everest in 2010. She also became the first British woman to summit Mount Lhotse, the world's fourth-highest mountain. Norris has completed several other expeditions, including a skiing expedition to the geographic North Pole, and climbing Mount Manaslu, Mount Ama Dablam and Mount Imja Tse. Outside of mountaineering and exploring, she has become an ambassador for countless educational institutions and a Patron of the White Lodge Disability Centre in Surrey.

JOY: A FEELING OF EXTREME GLADNESS, delight, or exaltation of the spirit arising from a sense of well-being or satisfaction.

The meaning of life for me is being connected to the trinity of nature, other & self. What I mean by that is, when we are deeply connected to nature, other beings and ourselves, we find we are living in the present moment – and it is in these moments of deep and present connection that we experience the most profound of all human emotions: joy.

Joy isn't just the feeling of happiness or gratitude, though these are part of it. Joy is a transcendental feeling of connection to something that matters to us – whether that is accomplishing something and feeling deeply connected to ourselves, making and sharing food with friends and feeling connected to others, or experiencing the power of nature. For me, it was aged 20, the clouds parting on the world's 6th highest peak, Mt Manaslu, and seeing the Himalayas spread out around me. That moment brought me to my knees in tears of joy. Ever since then, I have wondered what that powerful emotion was and why I experienced it. It was a sense that despite all the struggle I had been through on that mountain, I was right where I was supposed to be. It was a moment of spirituality and presence that I had not felt before.

Just after I became the youngest British female to reach the summit of Mt Everest in 2010, I received a message from a young girl who said she wanted to climb Everest and take my 'youngest British woman' record. 'Don't help her!' was the advice from family and friends, but I remembered the previous record holder, Tori James, who, when I was aspiring to take the accolade from her, met me in London and told me 'you will climb that mountain'. Now it was my turn to pass on the words that Tori had said to me. I mentored Becky and two years later when she came down from the summit of Everest, having successfully taken the record from me, it just so happened that I was at Everest base camp at the time, having been climbing Mt Lhotse, and I got to be the first person to embrace her when she reached camp. I can't describe the heart-bursting joy I felt in that moment as tears streamed from my eyes and my smile reached from ear to ear, and it struck me that that moment meant more to me than when I had stood on the summit of Everest myself.

Joy sometimes catches us by surprise: how is it that I felt more joy for the person who took a record from me, than for when I broke that record myself?

For our ancient ancestors, joy would have guided them through the hardships of life – by looking after one another, by trying to accomplish new things and by appreciating the beauty of the world around them, they would have found purpose and meaning in a world full of danger, trauma and threats. Seeking those deep and overwhelming feelings of joy would have kept them alive.

As their descendants – we're not living in daily life and death situations as our ancestors were, by contrast we live disconnected lives and experience profound loneliness and hopelessness at the lack of meaning the modern world gives us. We know something is wrong, and yet we find it hard to put our finger on. The truth is, urban environments do not spark joy, and neither does the disconnected way in which we live, where it is possible to go days without communicating with others much less experience a deep connection with another human being. Our culture of convenience means people don't understand the joy that comes from accomplishing something we have set our minds to, and so we become profoundly disconnected from the three things that bring us a deep sense of connection.

I hope to teach my children the importance of seeking connection to nature, other and self so that they too can connect to that most primal of emotions: joy, and I believe that when they find joy, whether that's in a piece of music, a mountain climb, a moment of deep connection with another human being, they will understand the meaning of life.

'Despite all the struggle I had been through on that mountain, I was right where I was supposed to be.'

ALEXANDER CAMPBELL

ALEXANDER CAMPBELL is currently walking around the world. In February 2023, he embarked on a four-year journey to circumnavigate the globe on foot, starting and ending in his hometown of Sydney, Australia. His chosen route will see him walk roughly 40,000km, through thirty countries, and across four continents. He's previously hiked the Colorado Trail (800km), across the entire length of Nepal on the Great Himalaya Trail (1,600km), and from the Flinders Ranges to Sydney (3,750km).

THE BEST WAY IN WHICH I know how to answer your question is to reflect on my own life and how I have sought to find meaning and purpose in it.

At this current moment, I find myself in Nepal, just over one year and 10,000km into a walk around the world. For me, long-distance hiking and adventure have played a defining role in bringing a sense of direction and fulfilment to my life.

Hiking has been a part of my life for almost a decade now. Since I was young, I was fascinated by adventurous forms of travel, whether it be hitchhiking, cycling or travelling on foot. And so once I finished high school and was finally set free, I took off on a ten-month trip during which I experimented with all forms of travel.

I went on my first ever multi-day hike with a friend in Hungary. On our first day walking, we ended up being invited into the home of some Hungarian farmers. They gave us a bed for the night and stuffed us full of meat and booze. And to our surprise, at 7 a.m. the following morning, they greeted us with a few more shots of spirits for breakfast before we set off walking for the day.

Over the course of my trip, I went on to hike in England, Morocco and Nepal. And while in India, I bought a second-hand bicycle for $10 and set off pedalling down the west coast for a few weeks. These adventures were tough, painful and scary at times, but they also filled me with a childlike sense of wonder and lust for life. And through firsthand experience it taught me that the vast majority of people in the world are kind, welcoming and will offer a helping hand. Ultimately, it lived up to my romantic vision of adventure and of the life I had fantasised of living.

I eventually returned home, started studying a Bachelor of Arts majoring in Anthropology and Archaeology at university and picked up a part-time job working in the warehouse of IKEA. Over the next few years, I managed to squeeze in a few adventures along the way, including hiking the 800km-long Colorado Trail while on my way to Montreal for a university exchange. This cemented my love for long-distance hiking and two years later I took a semester off to trek 1,600km across the entire length of Nepal.

I eventually ended up writing my honours thesis for Anthropology on the experiences and struggles of long-distance hikers reintegrating into life after their hike. After its completion and feeling burnt out from a stressful year behind the screen of my laptop, I set off on another big walk to recharge and reset. This time I hiked 3,750km from the Flinders Ranges to my home in Sydney; however, it was the first time in my life I came home without having university to automatically fall back into. And so upon my return, I had to stop and think, What now? What do I want to do with my life? After much pondering, the one thing that I knew I loved was going on these adventures and that they sparked within me a sense of excitement and appreciation for life that I haven't found elsewhere.

I began to imagine, What would my life look like if I went all in on this passion? And I started scheming possible multi-year adventures. When I finally concocted the idea to walk around the world and excitedly pitched my big new plan to my parents, I remember my mum observing me and saying, 'It's so nice to see that spark in your eye.' I'm so fortunate and grateful to have two parents that can recognise that spark and value it. It's always felt that as long as I'm passionate, happy and driven about what I'm doing, I know I'll have the support, love and backing of my parents, even if the path I'm choosing is a little unconventional. And this has meant the world to me.

In a journal entry from when I was eighteen years old and about to finish high school, I expressed my fear that I felt I had all this energy and potential, but I didn't know what to channel it into. I was afraid that I may never find that thing and would end up in some ways living an unlived life.

I believe that walking has become that thing I was searching for, which I can throw myself into wholeheartedly. To challenge myself both physically and mentally and hopefully learn and grow from those experiences and come out the other side a stronger, more competent and compassionate person.

I'm not sure what the meaning of my life will be after this walk is complete. But for now, having the clear path and direction it provides is extremely fulfilling and is one of the main reasons I love long-distance hiking. To wake up each morning and know exactly which direction I'm heading is a beautifully comforting thing.

I love the sense of fulfilment it provides, striving everyday towards a larger goal and being able to see clear tangible progress as I put one foot in front of the other.

I think this will be the main challenge after finishing my walk. Finding that new thing to set my compass towards and to centre my focus and efforts. Although I look forward to whatever that next adventure is, whether it be a new career, fatherhood or possibly someday another (not so) long walk.

What I hope one can take away from my ramblings is to lean into your passions and don't be afraid to dream. Embrace what challenges and excites you. It's a wonderful thing to be alive here on this big, beautiful world so do your best to enjoy the journey. Cherish those who support, appreciate and love you for the weird, imperfect person that we all are and provide the same for others, as we make our way together through this incredible thing called life.

All the best,

Alexander

DAVID
SMITH MBE

DAVID SMITH is an athlete, speaker and coach. He won a gold medal as part of the Team GB rowing squad at the London 2012 Paralympics. He was first diagnosed with cancerous tumours on his spinal cord in 2010, and although the journey to London 2012 ended in triumph, the cancer returned not once, but four more times. Smith, who was awarded an MBE in 2013 for services to rowing, has had multiple surgeries, one of which – in 2016 – left him paralysed down his left side.

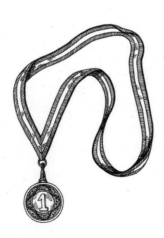

I'VE HAD FOURTEEN YEARS to reflect upon my own death so I've had a long time to reflect on what is the meaning of life, and to think about these kinds of questions. I've wrestled with them in ICU, and in cancer wards where I've seen people take their last breath and die. I've wrestled with the question of faith and where we go after this, and also the future of Homo sapiens, and the future of the planet. I would love to say after all this thinking that I have a definitive answer to this question!

I do know that as my life has evolved, my perception and how I would answer this question has also evolved. I think if you asked the young David Smith, in his early teenage years, it would have been about pleasure, hedonism, and about following what made me happy and what brought me joy. For some people that might be art, it might be music, it might be drinking and going to nightclubs. For me, for young David Smith, it was all about sport.

At first, it was the pleasure of playing with friends, but then my philosophy became very much attached to winning and performing at the highest level. I strived to win medals and be the best in the world at what I do.

My first cancer diagnosis came in 2010, and for the first time I was faced with my own mortality. But at that point, I was also two years out from the London Games, so my mind was still consumed with making it to an Olympics and becoming a World Champion.

Fast forward through fourteen years of cancer, seven spinal surgeries, and paralysis, and now death has become a part of my life. I came out of my last surgery some six and a half weeks ago, but the guy in the bed next to me chose to die. He was fifty-four, and he didn't want to try the three options to carry on living. He just went, 'You know what? I'm done.' As the nurse was preparing him for end of life, she asked him what his faith was to which he replied: 'Faith, I just want to be made comfortable, turn off all the machines, and I'll just go.' And then she came in and cleaned his little bay out, wiped his name off the wall. And that was it, he was gone.

Since coming out of hospital, I've been watching about the evolution of life. You could argue at the rawest level of Darwin's natural selection that the meaning is ultimately to keep the species going. In an animal kingdom you find your partner, you procreate, you produce more Homo sapiens and the race goes on. I think if we looked back to Homo erectus, and even to the Neanderthal years, it was again just about survival, about procreating, and keeping the species going. Yet as I watched this, I thought to myself if the meaning of life is purely just to procreate and keep the human species going then where do I fit in?

Therefore, rather than looking at life as a whole, and wondering what is the meaning of Homo sapiens on this planet, I then started thinking, What's the meaning of David Smith's life?

I realised that whilst winning a medal and competing at the highest level were great achievements, they're but a fleeting moment in time. One of the dangers we have as humans is that we live either in the past or in the future. We struggle to live in the present moment.

In fact, I remember waking up six months after winning my medal, and nothing had really changed. The more diagnoses I had, and the more I wrestled with mortality, I started to look at the history of sports people and I realised that you're actually forgotten about pretty quickly. Some people will want to live off of a medal and identify as a world champion for the rest of their life, but it was only a moment in time. You can ask young athletes: who was the 1908 Olympic champion in the 400 metres? Hardly anyone knows, unless you're a historian. Even in your own family, if I had to ask somebody who their great, great, great, great grandfather was and what did he do? Many people can't answer that question. Even if you just go back to your great grandfather, many people can't answer that question either. So I think if you're doing anything purely for an external gratification, driven by the ego, I think that's a dangerous pursuit.

Now, as I sit a little bit older – and I'd like to say a little bit wiser – and as I come closer to death, I realise that sport is something I do. It's a part of my identity. But it's not who I am. I'm also a son, and a partner. I have a great love of philosophy and of psychology. Likewise, I don't identify purely as a cancer sufferer, or with having a disability. It's something I have, but it's not who I am.

The danger with identifying as one thing is when you wake up in a hospital bed, fighting for your life, you no longer have that identity, and you have to work out who you are. I was a six-foot-four, 100-kilo rower, and then I became a disabled person using a wheelchair, who is super vulnerable. I personally don't want to attach to either of those identities because I'm more than both of those physical identities. So, in a very spiritual way I'm more than the body I'm in.

In the spinal cord hospital you're known as your injury. So I was known as tetraplegic Asia D. And that was it. People would come up to me and ask, 'What are you?' You wouldn't say, 'I'm David Smith, I'm an athlete.' You say, 'I'm tetraplegic Asia D', which is crazy.

It's like when you meet somebody, one of the very first questions is always: What do you do? And then from your answer the other person through a cognitive bias will create a judgement in their mind of who you are as a person. Are you part of their tribe? Or are you of any use to their tribe? And the conversation can end basically on the answer of what you do. I hate that. And instead I often try to ask what people's passions are, what drives them, what their dreams are, what they do in their spare time, and then I get a real insight to who this person is.

Personally, my passions are being in nature, making a difference, helping to inspire and motivate people, and doing sport and moving my body. And if I do all of those things, then I'm happy.

Knowing that I am going to die, I wake up each morning with a high level of gratitude that I've just opened my eyes. I've been blessed to see a sunrise, and hopefully I'll see the sunset. I've found peace and contentment in the simplest things. I don't have to go and ski off a double-black diamond run any more, I can just wake up and taste my coffee. One of the great lessons of being paralysed but yet being able to walk is that I have to be in the present moment for every step I take – I have to be conscious or I fall over. So I've managed to teach myself just be in the present moment, and with that, I find happiness is a byproduct.

I like to think of life as chapters in a book. And when one chapter closes, you read a new one.

Now I want to try and share my experiences from the cancer wards, from looking at my own mortality, to thinking how can I help my fellow humans live a more flourishing life where they experience more joy, more happiness, and potentially less suffering.

'Knowing that I'm going to die, I wake up each morning with a high level of gratitude that I've just opened my eyes.'

YUSUF / CAT STEVENS

JESSE TYLER FERGUSON

RACHEL PORTMAN OBE

SIR MICHAEL EAVIS

SANANDA MAITREYA

RUTH ROGERS CBE

LUKE JERRAM

STEFAN SAGMEISTER

TOMMY CANNON

THE CONNOR BROTHERS

DAVID HURN

MAX FOSH

JONATHAN GOODWIN

JOAN ARMATRADING CBE

Artists & Entertainers

YUSUF /
CAT STEVENS

YUSUF / CAT STEVENS is a singer-songwriter and musician who has sold more than 100 million records and has more than two billion streams. His 1967 debut album and its title song 'Matthew and Son' both reached the top 10 in the UK charts. Stevens's albums *Tea for the Tillerman* (1970) and *Teaser and the Firecat* (1971) were certified triple platinum in the US. His 1972 album *Catch Bull at Four* went on to reach number one on the Billboard 200. His hit songs include 'The First Cut is the Deepest', 'Father and Son' and 'Wild World'. He was inducted into the Rock and Roll Hall of Fame in 2014.

TRUTH IS, NONE OF US ASKED to be here. So what is the purpose of breathing and being alive? To seek out and find the meaning of life should be everybody's aim. And I certainly made that my job before time ran out.

I once wrote a song called 'On the Road to Find Out', that song was a metaphor for Life itself, and the future was basically going to be a journey of discovery; it was written soon after my battle with TB, at the age of nineteen. That was the first time I had to face up to my own weakness and mortal limits.

While being treated in hospital, I had been given a book to read to help pass the time, it was called *The Secret Path*. It was exactly what I needed. That book began my enquiry into the question of 'self' and 'being'. There were a lot of questions, but without doubt the greatest mystery was in connection with the unseen – and what might lie beyond the door of death?

It was because of that disturbing question I was desperate to look beyond life's mundane issues and study various paths concerned with the spirit. Having been educated in a strict Catholic school, it was liberating to look deeper into 'other' religions, like Buddhism, Zen, Taoism – and even as far as Numerology. That metaphysical journey led me to the discovery of the Qur'an in 1975. This was where answers began to arise and form clearly in front of me.

Words and meanings flew at me from every existential angle. The stories and parables within many chapters of this book seemed to be a continuation of Christian-Judaeo narrative, but the meanings seemed to have evolved. There was a brightness and clarity I had never experienced before, when reading the Bible.

The story of Adam was here! But the events which unfolded around his creation led to a completely new understanding about what it means to be human. Whereas before, there was always the problem of 'original sin'. Here the story explained a vital secret: Adam was created to 'learn'.

'And God taught Adam the names of all things . . .'[1]

Following this initial instruction, both man and woman were given the freedom to live and dwell in the Garden of Paradise, but God warned them never to eat from a particular tree. That meant they had to make choices. As things turned out, Adam and Eve disregarded the order which they were given, and fell for Satan's trick. But all was not lost! They had learned a great lesson! Now they were sent to live on Earth. But, importantly here, God promised to send them words of guidance:

'And whoever follows my guidance, shall not fear nor sorrow . . .'[2]

The clearest difference between human beings and animals is the inner conscience within us. Ours is essentially a life of moral choices. The decisions we make fulfill our purpose and lead us to our destiny, either good or bad. Fortunately, we are not left to make up the rules of life ourselves. That's where Revelation and Prophets and Messengers provide the link.

So, in summary: I believe we have all been especially invited here to this majestic Kingdom of the One God, in His boundless universe. We have been graciously placed on this most beautiful planet, full of natural wonders, with fruits, nourishment, family and companions, its green carpet laid out with rivers and mountains, a roof of blue blowing silver clouds, and a golden star above us to keep us warm. We live on a spherical

---

[1] The Qur'an 2:31

[2] The Qur'an 2:38

floating home, suspended in the midst of the majestic heavens, full of stars and billions of galaxies. All this for free, without cost.

Or, perhaps not. There's a catch to this beautiful scenario: we all have to die! Before we do, our hearts are confronted with options, some of which are good and some of which are bad. If we choose too many bad ones, we spoil our chances to be invited back to the Garden of Paradise, to enjoy an infinitely more joyful life of endless gifts and surprises, expanding our freedom to do as we wish any way we please, with no 'tree' off limits and nothing nasty or bothersome to interfere with our happiness.

So be warned. If we choose wrongly, we will unfortunately be led to a place with the worst of company, cramped and restricted, where everything is disgusting and painful and we have no choice or chance to ever walk out and leave. So be wise, think carefully, act right, and choose well.

In the end, the words of my song 'On The Road To Find Out' were in perfect tune with Divine destiny. So, I will end it here – and leave you to work the rest out.

'Yes, the answer lies within, why not take a look now?

Kick out the devil's sin, pick up, pick up a good book now!'[3]

Yusuf Cat Stevens

---

[3] 'On The Road To Find Out', *Tea for the Tillerman*, 1970

JESSE TYLER FERGUSON

JESSE TYLER FERGUSON is an actor who portrayed Mitchell Pritchett in the sitcom *Modern Family*, for which he earned five consecutive nominations for the Primetime Emmy Award for Outstanding Supporting Actor in a Comedy Series. Ferguson was awarded a Drama Desk Award for Outstanding Solo Performance for his performance in the 2016 Broadway production of *Fully Committed*, and won the Tony Award for Best Featured Actor in a Play for his performance in the 2022 Broadway revival of *Take Me Out*. He is also the founder of the charity 'Pronoun', which exists to advocate for the civil rights of the LGBTQIA+ community in the United States and beyond.

JAMES -

WHAT AN INTERESTING
QUESTION THAT I HAVE
NEVER BEEN ASKED.
LIFE IS A PRIVILAGE
FOR ME - SOMETHING
THAT ISN'T EARNED
BUT ALSO NOT JUST
GIVEN. I FEEL LUCKY
TO LIVE IT IN THE
MOMENT I AM IN.
NOW, I'M A DAD SO
LIFE IS A LIFE RAFT

FOR MY ~~KIDS~~ KIDS.
LIFE IS A PLAYGROUND
AND A SCHOOL AND
A BLUEPRINT FOR
THEM. IT FEELS
LESS MINE AND
MORE SOMETHING I
PROTECT FOR THEM.
LIFE IS SOMETHING I'M
IN CUSTODY OF!
         Xo.
      JESSE TYLER FERGUSON

WHAT AN INTERESTING QUESTION that I have never been asked. Life is a privilege for me – something that isn't earned but also not just given. I feel lucky to live it in the moment I am in. Now, I'm a dad so life is a life raft for my kids. Life is a playground and a school and a blueprint for them. It feels less mine and more something I protect for them. Life is something I'm in custody of!

RACHEL PORTMAN OBE

RACHEL PORTMAN is a composer who, in 1996, became the first female composer to win an Academy Award, which she received for the score of *Emma*. She was also the first female composer to win a Primetime Emmy Award, which she received for the film *Bessie*. She has received two further Academy Nominations for *The Cider House Rules* and *Chocolat*, and has also written stage and concert works, among them commissions from the BBC Proms and Houston Grand Opera.

Meaning of Life

I would like to leave life having made a difference, however small, to others whether through my music, by listening or love.

Those are the three things that bring most meaning and nourishment to my life.

A while ago I spent two years working very closely with Saint-Exupéry's The Little Prince, writing an opera on it. I was deeply affected by the story. My experience was a synthesis of absorbing the book's themes for an extended period, expressing them musically in my own language and then the realisation of the opera itself in which the performers were again moved by the story's message and in turn passed it to the audience. The experience was a very meaningful one.

"One sees clearly only with the heart."

I find meaning too in small things and those moments around the edges of life, where a brief connection with someone happens, something intimate is shared or a friend opens up a door to their inner world.

In composing, what fulfils me most is to be able through music to connect with others and though it's sometimes tough to write, what I really want is to move people and for a moment, for them to feel the beauty of the earth, or the trees and rivers. I seem for whatever reason to constantly want to bring emotion to others through my music and increasingly this is through themes of the earth as well as love and connection.

My personal relationships bring me much fulfilment - my three daughters, my family, friends and my wonderful husband.

I had therapy for several years and even trained as a psychotherapist as a result. It brought me closer to understanding how to find meaning in my life and to help others to do the same.

So these would be my thoughts on the
meaning of my life —

to learn to be whole
to learn to love completely
to learn to receive love
to learn to be congruent
to be with and appreciate birds, trees
                                    and the earth

to care for others
to listen carefully
to see clearly with the heart
to be at one with my soul

to make music that moves

Rachel Portman

I WOULD LIKE TO LEAVE life having made a difference, however small, to others, whether through my music, by listening or love.

Those are the three things that bring most meaning and nourishment to my life.

A while ago I spent two years working very closely with Saint-Exupéry's *The Little Prince*, writing an opera on it. I was deeply affected by the story. My experience was a synthesis of absorbing the book's themes for an extended period, expressing them musically in my own language and then the realisation of the opera itself in which the performers were again affected by the message of the story and in turn passed it to the audience. The experience was a very meaningful one.

'One sees clearly only with the heart.'

I find meaning too in small things and those moments around the edges of life, where a brief connection with someone happens, something intimate is shared or a friend opens up a door into their inner world.

In composing, what fulfils me most is to be able through music to connect with others and though it's sometimes tough to write, what I really want is to move people and for a moment for them to feel the beauty of the earth, or the trees, and rivers. I seem for whatever reason to constantly want to bring emotion to others through my music and increasingly this is through themes of the earth as well as love and connection.

My personal relationships bring me much fulfilment – my three daughters, close family, friends and my wonderful husband.

I had therapy for several years and even trained as a psychotherapist as a result. It brought me closer to understanding how to find meaning in my life and to help others to do the same.

So these would be my thoughts on the meaning of my life –
To learn to be whole
To learn to love completely
To learn to receive love
To learn to be congruent
To be with and appreciate birds, trees and the earth
To care for others
To listen carefully
To see clearly with the heart
To be at one with my soul
To make music that moves

Sir
MICHAEL EAVIS

SIR MICHAEL EAVIS is the owner of Worthy Farm and the co-founder of Glastonbury Festival. Inspired by watching Led Zeppelin's performance at the Bath Festival of Blues in 1969, the following year Eavis hosted the Pilton Pop Folk & Blues Festival. In 1971 the Glastonbury Fayre was organised, and this later developed into the Glastonbury Festival. Today, the festival is regarded as a major event in British culture, and is attended by approximately 200,000 people. Headliners have included Sir Paul McCartney, David Bowie, the Rolling Stones, Kanye West, Beyoncé, Jay-Z, Oasis, Adele and Billie Eilish. Eavis appeared on stage himself in 2010 with Stevie Wonder, and in 2016, at the age of eighty, he accompanied Coldplay on stage in a rendition of 'My Way'.

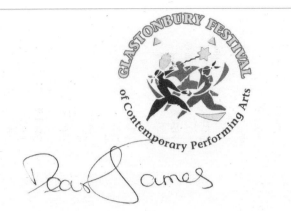

09/04/18

Thank you for your letter. A most reasonable and considered response from me goes like this:

It's taken millions of years for mankind, particularly humans, to get to the point we're at now. That creates a real value to life.

The process of living takes a lot of time planning, loving, eating and enjoying pleasurable pursuits like music, sport, artistic achievements, raising kids and teaching them to mix with their peers so that they can feel joyful about being alive and kicking!

However, for those who are not able or willing to fit into my fairly normal way of existing, then there's another way perhaps to find happiness and joy through seeking a path to spirituality. Millions upon millions of people across the world get huge joy from reaching 'Nirvana' and being in close contact with who they believe to be their creator, or even their God.

On that quasi-religious note, I was brought up a Methodist and to use whatever talent and resources one has to improve the quality of life for others less fortunate than ourselves.

Yours sincerely,

supporting **GREENPEACE** 🅰 OXFAM 🅰 WaterAid *and other worthwhile causes*

Glastonbury Festivals Ltd., Worthy Farm, Pilton, Shepton Mallet, Somerset BA4 4BY *(Registered office)*

VAT Nº 601 0982 76

Registered in England and Wales • Company no. 2737866

THANK YOU FOR YOUR LETTER. A most reasonable and considered response from me goes like this:

It's taken millions of years for mankind, particularly humans, to get to the point we're at now. That creates real value to life.

The process of living takes a lot of time planning, loving, eating and enjoying pleasurable pursuits like music, sport, artistic achievements, raising kids and teaching them to mix with their peers so that they can feel joyful about being alive and kicking!

However, for those who are not able or willing to fit into my fairly normal way of existing, then there's another way perhaps to find happiness and joy through seeking a path to spirituality. Millions upon millions of people across the world get huge joy from reaching 'Nirvana' and being in close contact with who they believe to be their creator, or even their God.

On that quasi-religious note, I was brought up Methodist and to use whatever talent and resources one has to improve the quality of life for others less fortunate than ourselves.

Yours sincerely,
Michael Eavis

'It's taken millions
of years for man-
kind to get to the
point we're at now.
That creates a real
value to life.'

SANANDA MAITREYA

SANANDA MAITREYA, formerly known as Terence Trent D'Arby, is an acclaimed American singer, songwriter and multi-instrumentalist known for his groundbreaking debut album *Introducing the Hardline*, which included the hit singles 'Sign Your Name' and 'Wishing Well'. His versatile career spans decades, blending rock, pop and R&B, earning him accolades such as a Grammy and a BRIT Award. Maitreya's diverse discography showcases influences from funk, jazz and electronica, culminating in his 2024 album *The Pegasus Project: Pegasus & The Swan*. Renowned for his soulful vocals and innovative style, he also advocates for social causes and artistic expression.

FOR THE OUTLOOK THAT ACCOMPANIES my ever evolving process through these tunnels of the space time continuum as we perceive it, THE MEANING OF LIFE IS WHAT YOU DETERMINE THAT IT IS.

LIFE IS FLEXIBLE, because the Nature of its Shape isn't FIXED.

So, if you NEED Life to show YOU what it is, it is willing to play along, as it functions as a MIRROR, as much as it functions as anything else besides. YET, it is equally capable of taking a BACK SEAT & letting YOU DRIVE the vehicle that she, Life is.

Naturally you can join organizations or groups & allow THEM to give you THEIR proscribed definition of what Life is & isn't OR you can dismiss ALL OF THAT & collaborate with the Spirit that infuses Life & INVENT as well as REINVENT the form of consciousness as you travel on towards the Roads that Beckon. Along the way OTHER SYMPATHETIC PHILOSOPHIES can assist & comfort but eventually it is the faith that consciousness has in us that WE COME TO AWAKEN to the POWER WITHIN ourselves to realize THAT WE ARE CREATORS MADE IN THE 'IMAGE OF OUR FATHER' & make of our existence the fusion of our dreams & will.

End of Part 1 !

Part 2:

As it concerns the Native Tribes from which I stem, we don't believe in 'Death'.

Because for us, THERE IS NO DEATH ! It is a Western Construct & very much a means of Spirit Dominance & Mind Control. An essential part of the Laws of Basic Physics is that ENERGY CANNOT BE KILLED OR DIE, IT CAN ONLY BE TRANSFORMED into but another shape of Life, & to us, ALL THERE IS, IS LIFE. Much of it far beyond our stable frequencies capacity to comprehend. And we don't get to define what Life is to LIFE ITSELF.

The greater fear for the Soul isn't 'Death', IT IS LIFE !

So our greatest MEDITATION is in working through the 'Mystery of Life' to come to terms with US as our own MASTER. LIFE FOLLOWS AS WE GO. If seen through the predominant eyes of fear, then NATURALLY LIFE becomes an exercise in 'exorcising' fear. Then again, FEAR IS EXCITING, & highly seductive, so we've EVERY GOD GIVEN RIGHT to work with & through it until WE become bored & ready to move beyond it.

We are of course CONTROLLED THROUGH FEAR, a most valuable asset, UNTIL we are not. And it's why fear is peddled so readily, because it's cohesive & IT WORKS.

Societies & Organizations are bound by & with it, so it performs a very useful function on behalf of those who DERIVE THEIR POWER FROM OUR SURRENDER OF IT. Misery loves company & fear loves a cause.

And since 'Merrily Life Is But A Dream', once ready to awaken from the Fear Game, we then allow ourselves to remember that 'WHO DARES WINS', & are placed by our faith in a position to begin dreaming OUR DREAM & write the screenplays of our OWN DRAMAS.

AS FOR ME PERSONALLY it's just a matter of appreciating that I don't need to EAT ALL OF MY HONEY NOW, & I can also be patient & wait for the BITTER FRUITS TO RIPEN into the Sweetness that our Lives & Work have Earned us the right to anticipate. After all WE ARE GRANTED ALL THE TIME IN THE WORLD THAT WE NEED, & is in fact the only reason that TIME exists in the shape that it takes in our denser physical dimensions.

For indeed 'TIME IS ON MY SIDE'.

End of Part 2 !

Part 3:

THE PURPOSE REVEALS ITSELF AS WE GO, it unfolds, OR we make it what we'd have of it. The FULFILLMENT is in knowing that THE WORK WILL ALWAYS BE AVAILABLE to those willing to DO THE WORK. WE ARE NEVER FINISHED (until we SAY we are) & THAT IS THE GOOD NEWS ! The Orchards Remain & when our day is done, we return home to 'clean up' & replenish through REST & REFLECTION.

EVERY ASPECT OF OUR LIVING IS A MEDITATION, & all the more compelling when CONSCIOUSLY SO. And if we wish to continue riding the waves of this life, we return as often as we still maintain interest therein. Once we're ready to remain beyond the veils of this illusion, we move on to where our interest lies, BECAUSE ALL THERE IS, IS LIFE & more of it. We are given all of the 'Horses' that we require, but WE are the Driver of the Team & NOT THE HORSES. And gaining control of our team of Horses, of our Gifts & 'Demons', is a considerable portion of the great fascination that keeps us tethered to this 'Mortal Coil'. And made ALL THE EASIER & more fulfilling when we dare to STOP JUDGING WHO WE ARE, IN THE PROCESS OF SELF REALIZATION.

FOR THE REALIZATION & REMEMBRANCE OF WHO WE ARE, & the FORGIVENESS that we find along the way as we awaken from our sleep, is the main purpose of WHY WE ARE HERE & WHAT LIFE MEANS TO US. For, as we discover ourselves, so do we likewise discover LIFE, WE ARE LIFE & every fucking thing in it. Life is NOT GREATER THAN YOU, unless you INSIST that it is.

End Of Story !

Sananda Maitreya!

Wednesday 28 June '23

Milano, Italia!

RUTH
ROGERS CBE

RUTH ROGERS, Baroness Rogers of Riverside, is a chef who owns and runs the Michelin-starred Italian restaurant the River Café in Hammersmith, London. She was appointed Member of the Order of the British Empire (MBE) in the 2010 New Year Honours and Commander of the Order of the British Empire (CBE) in the 2020 Birthday Honours for services to the culinary arts and charity. She is the widow of the Italian-born British architect Richard Rogers, Baron Rogers of Riverside.

I WAS THE YOUNGEST OF THREE SIBLINGS, and came from a very small town in upstate New York. My parents always had a lot of time and energy for me, and I think, from a young age, that made me feel that life is all about people, and the connection I have with these people. Whether that is my family, my friends, people I've worked with, or simply people I meet in a shop, in a taxi, or in the street.

This focus on people has continued throughout my life. I went to a high school that was very much based on a philosophy of community. And then I came to London and was enveloped in Richard's world and his Italian family – I had three stepchildren at the very young age of just twenty-two. (Now with this extended family, I have thirteen grandchildren.)

When we moved into the neighbourhood of Chelsea, we wanted to get involved in the community – whether that was through the local theatre or a homeless shelter – and I also think this is why I've always been interested in political and social issues. It's been about how people are affected, whether by violence or unfairness.

Even in our work, Richard was an architect who really focused on the effect of his architecture on community and people. And when I became a chef and opened The River Café, it was an open-kitchen restaurant based on the ethics and values of creating a world that found meaning through its people (as well as serving really great food!). Hopefully, to this day it gives pleasure to both the people who are eating and the people who are cooking.

Home has also always been very important to me, as I grew up in a home with comfort. So as much as I enjoy to travel, I always want to come home.

LUKE JERRAM

LUKE JERRAM is an installation artist, who creates sculptures, large artwork installations and live arts projects. His artwork *Museum of the Moon*, a spherical model of the Moon, has been exhibited more than 300 times in thirty countries across the world; *Play Me I'm Yours* installed over 1,900 street pianos in seventy cities worldwide, and *Park and Slide* installed a giant water slide in Bristol. In 2023 alone, he had over 115 exhibitions in twenty-seven different countries, visited by more than three million people. Jerram's artworks are in over sixty permanent collections around the world, including the Metropolitan Museum of Art in New York, the Shanghai Museum of Glass, and the Wellcome Collection in London.

THANKS FOR GETTING IN TOUCH.

Big question here!!

Meaning from life for me comes in the connections with people I meet and through the experience people have with my artwork.

I enjoy giving joy to others and it's always lovely to hear the stories people tell me of their encounters they have with my work.

My arts project *Play Me I'm Yours* involves installing dozens of street pianos across cities for people to play. Several strangers have met each other over a street piano, fallen in love, and got married as a consequence. One couple even invited me to their wedding where they had the street piano that brought them together on display!

In 2013 I met Italian pianist Samuele Rossini who had arrived in London with nothing, homeless and looking for work. Samuele explained how when he first arrived in London by train, there was a piano just waiting for him at St Pancras International Station. Playing each day at the station, he was spotted by a producer who commissioned his first album!

In a train station in Sao Paulo, I came across a girl sitting at a piano with her mother in tears. It turns out the mother had worked as a cleaner for four years so her daughter could have piano lessons on the other side of town. As a piano costs a years wage they couldn't afford their own so this was the first time the mother had ever heard her daughter play! It was a beautiful moment and a privilege to witness it. The train station loved the project so much, they put pianos in all the other stations across the city.

As we speak, I'm now in Kerala, India, where last night we installed

The Museum of the Moon, a 7m-diameter replica of the Moon made of NASA imagery. Over 100,000 people descended on the park last night to see the Moon. It was crazy and I needed bouncers to escort me out of the mass of people and press. One young girl asked me there, 'Will you put the Moon back afterwards?' I reassured her that I would definitely put the Moon back in the sky after that evening.

I love giving these unusual and hopefully joyful experiences to others, and hope to carry on doing so, as long as I can.

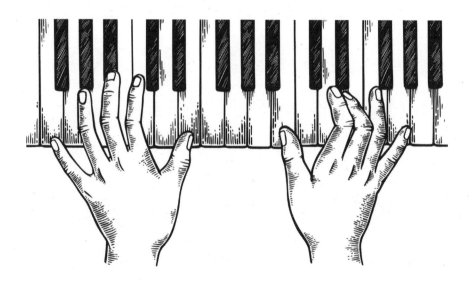

'Meaning from life for me comes in the connections with people I meet and through the experience people have with my artwork.'

STEFAN SAGMEISTER

STEFAN SAGMEISTER is a graphic designer, storyteller and typographer based in New York City. In 1993, Sagmeister founded his company, Sagmeister Inc., to create designs for the music industry. Since then he has won three Grammy Awards, and designed album covers for Lou Reed, OK Go, the Rolling Stones, David Byrne, Jay-Z, Aerosmith, Talking Heads and Brian Eno. His documentary *The Happy Film* premiered at the Tribeca Film Festival 2016, and explored his ten-year exploration of happiness. Sagmeister curated the accompanying exhibition, *The Happy Show*, which was displayed at the Museum of Contemporary Art, Los Angeles.

Hello JAMES,

I FIND MY <u>WORK</u> COMES TO
BE MEANINGFUL WHEN IT IS
ABLE TO HELP & DELIGHT
OTHER PEOPLE.

IN MY <u>LIFE</u>, I CAN
TRY TO LIFT ALL MY RELATIONSHIPS,
- the CLOSE ones & THE NOT SO CLOSE
ONES — ONTO A LEVEL HIGH
ENOUGH THAT LITTLE HAPPINESSES
CAN COME OUT from IN-BETWEEN —
WHEN I DONT EXPECT them & WITHOUT
ME PURSUING THEM.

I CAN TRY to ACHIEVE
the SAME WITH MY WORK
& WITH SOMETHING BIGGER THAN
MYSELF.

IF I'M ABLE to
to THAT, MY LIFE WILL
HAVE MEANING.

much love from
NEW YORK,
Stefan
Sagmeister

I FIND MY WORK GETS to be meaningful when it is able to help and delight other people.

In my life, I can try to lift all my relationships – the close ones and the not so close ones – onto a level high enough that little happinesses can come out from in-between – when I don't expect them and without me pursuing them.

I can try to achieve the same with my work and with something bigger than myself.

If I'm able to do that, my life will have meaning.

Much love from New York,

Stefan Sagmeister

TOMMY CANNON

TOMMY CANNON is a comedian, best known for his double-act partnership with Bobby Ball as Cannon & Ball. Gaining success in northern working men's clubs, they first appeared on television in 1968 on the talent show *Opportunity Knocks*. The duo landed their own prime-time Saturday-night television series, *The Cannon and Ball Show*, in the 1980s, which ran for nine years and had an average audience of twenty million viewers.

THE MEANING OF LIFE FOR ME would be to be happy.

I know that sounds cheesy, however it's so important to be happy in whatever you do and if it's not bringing you happiness there is something wrong or you shouldn't do it.

I'm a big believer in everything happens for a reason and life gives you a path to follow – you may fall off the path, and it may go in different directions but you will always get back on that path.

Family is one of the most important things for me, that's how I fulfil my life and what gives me purpose, the love of my family, how I can talk to them and be heard.

My whole life has been centred around laughter in my job, and I couldn't live without laughter, it's like a language.

THE CONNOR
BROTHERS

THE CONNOR BROTHERS is the pseudonym for artists Mike Snelle and James Golding. Their work, which delves into contemporary issues – including social media, politics and fake news – has been exhibited internationally and can be found in major public and private collections. They are best known for reinterpreting objects from the past and providing a humorous twist on contemporary obsession with wealth, fame and the unrealistic idealism of human relationships.

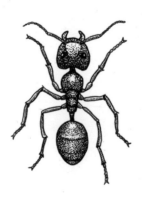

HUMANKIND'S SEARCH FOR MEANING is an unfortunate evolutionary anomaly amongst the animal kingdom, and the myriad attempts to create meaning where there is none is responsible for more suffering and violence than anything else. We're really not that important. You don't find trees thinking fucking hell, what's the point in all this, or rocks starting wars over their belief in their unique and superior place in the natural order. Even the question what does life mean betrays our inability to accept we are no different from any other living creature, and that our lives have no more significance than a mosquito's. Accepting that life is meaningless, allows space for acknowledging we are part of the unique, miraculous and fragile ecosystem that is life on earth, and maybe then we can start protecting it rather than destroying it in our maniacal bid for species domination. Even, or especially, in a world without meaning we should strive to be kind, to each other and to the unbelievably rich world in which we are privileged to play a minor role. The greatest joy can be found not in the search for meaning but in the noticing and being fully part of the natural world.

DAVID HURN

DAVID HURN is a documentary photographer, member of Magnum Photos, and the founder of Newport's School of Documentary Photography. He gained his reputation for his documentation of the Hungarian revolution of 1956, before working on a number of large film and television sets, taking publicity shots of Sean Connery for the Bond film *From Russia with Love,* and spending seven weeks photographing The Beatles during the filming of *A Hard Day's Night.* Among many other stars, he has photographed Sophia Loren, Audrey Hepburn, Jane Fonda, Michael Caine, Vanessa Redgrave, Peter O'Toole and Al Pacino. His long and varied career has also taken in some key moments in history, including the Aberfan disaster.

I HAVE NO REAL BELIEFS in any religion therefore do not have the comfort of being able to prepare for an afterlife, but I have questioned myself as to 'is there a point of being here?' and if so, what is it?

I have had rewarding experiences, love – which I don't understand but like – and friendship which is so difficult to explain, but hopefully it's someone with whom you can be yourself.

I also know that my life has been enhanced by persons from the past and present from whom I frequently steal, I call it inspiration – Turner, Bruegel, Bach, Verdi, Schubert, Montaigne, Orwell, Jan Morris, Marie Curie, Cartier Bresson, Koudelka. Each, and of course so many more, have enriched and coloured my life.

What they all have in common is that they enjoyed a personal activity that can continue to have a life after them – dependent on many variables, what they achieved could live for ever.

My passion, non fiction photography, performs one function supremely well: it shows what something or somebody looked like, under a particular set of conditions at a particular moment in time. This specificity has been, and remains, photography's boon as well as its bane. It's an interpretation of the real, it is a trace – something directly stencilled off the real, like a footprint in the snow. As what I do to make a living can fall into the criteria of having a future life, maybe my purpose is to attempt to do what I do as well as I can, with no compromise with honesty, exactness, and subjectity/objectivity, so the future can see, however imperfectly, what one person in the past saw/felt/loved.

MAX FOSH

MAX FOSH is a YouTuber and comedian who boasts more than three million subscribers, and whose videos have been watched more than 300 million times across all platforms. He is best known for his silly pranks, which have seen him become the richest man in the world for seven minutes, become a member of the Royal Family, sneak into London Fashion Week, purchase his own airline, buy a roundabout, and even run for London Mayor. In 2021, Fosh went on a nationwide tour, performing his stand-up comedy show, *Zocial Butterfly*, which he also took to the Edinburgh Fringe in 2022.

THANKS FOR THINKING OF ME FOR THIS.

My answer to this is quite simple: For me the meaning of life is connection with others.

We come into this world with nothing and we leave with nothing and so in the eighty years in which we are here it's about experiencing the deepest connections that we can. Humans are very social creatures and so if you look at anything that people like, you could argue it's all because these hobbies/interests bind us with our fellow man. Religion, sports, music all serve one and the same purpose.

I was very privileged to grow up in a home that had ample food on the table and the occasional trip to the South of France. From the outset, I had everything but in my early life, I was a very angry little boy. I think a lot of that stemmed from a feeling that I hadn't quite found MY group of peers.

This all changed when I went to university. Being in a dank, leaky university halls was the happiest that I felt as I was surrounded by people I could connect with.

As those relationships began to flourish, it gave me clarity that my purpose on this earth was to form relationships. We have seen from medical experiments that show that loneliness is so dangerous. 'Women who described themselves as lonely were three times more likely to die within a year of a heart attack than those with an active social life' (*Telegraph* 2019).

Therefore, go out and try and make connections where you can.

Connections in the South of France also work. ;)

Cheers, Max

JONATHAN GOODWIN

JONATHAN GOODWIN is a retired stunt performer, escape artist and daredevil. His dangerous stunts took him to the final of *Britain's Got Talent*, and the semi-final of *America's Got Talent*. In October 2021, Goodwin was hospitalised following injuries sustained during a stunt rehearsal for *America's Got Talent: Extreme*. The stunt was supposed to see Goodwin escape a straitjacket while upside-down 30 feet in the air, suspended between two cars. Instead, he became crushed between the cars as they caught fire. He was released from hospital in February 2022 but was left paralysed from the waist down, requiring the use of a wheelchair.

JAMES, FIRST OF ALL I'M IMMENSELY FLATTERED to be asked for an opinion on what is considered by many to be a very weighty topic. I think it's a uniquely human trait to try and assign meaning not just to existence but to all manner of things in life. I think it comes from a fundamental lack of understanding. If you go back in history we know that when it thundered or if the crops failed the people assumed it meant the gods were angry. Now we know that isn't the case and even the idea of assigning meaning to something as arbitrary as thunder seems a little ridiculous. I think that trying to find a meaning for life is just as ridiculous; and if I might venture further, it is a waste of precious time. It's a bit like standing in the middle of a beautiful forest and not noticing how gorgeous your surroundings are because you are too busy looking for something called a tree. The moment in my life that I stopped searching for meaning and became content to just exist in an incredible world was the same moment I really understood who I was.

In 2021 I was injured in a stunt accident which left me paralysed. I was hanging thirty feet in the air and was crushed between two cars, which exploded, and then I fell headfirst to the ground. I broke both my legs, suffered massive third-degree burns, destroyed a kidney, broke my ribs, punctured a lung, broke both my shoulders and suffered a complete spinal injury. I should have died twice (once in the accident and the second time on the operating table). My life entirely changed in an instant. It was an unimaginable loss; and I use the world unimaginable in its truest sense, as the journey that you undertake when you experience a spinal injury is little discussed and extremely arduous. It's odd then, that lying in my hospital bed having been told I would never walk again, I didn't experience a sense of loss but a feeling of great fortune. I am so incredibly lucky to be here, to have survived; to be able to sit in my kitchen two years later, with my dog Buster on my lap and write this for you. I pinch myself every single day and take great pleasure in the smallest moments because that is where the real beauty in life lies for me. The great fortune that I feel now was not one which was bestowed upon me in a terrible accident, but one that I always had and just didn't appreciate.

It is a fortune that also belongs to every single person reading this. Life doesn't need a meaning because existence in itself is magical enough. Nearly dying is an incredible therapy but just not one which I would recommend.

'Nearly dying is
an incredible
therapy but just
not one which
I would
recommend.'

JOAN
ARMATRADING CBE

JOAN ARMATRADING is a singer-songwriter and guitarist. A three-time Grammy Award nominee, Armatrading has also been nominated twice for BRIT Awards as Best Female Artist. She received an Ivor Novello Award for Outstanding Contemporary Song Collection in 1996.

THE MEANING OF LIFE IS TO
'Do Stuff'.
That's why we are here.

SIR JOHN MAJOR KG CH

PRESIDENT JIMMY CARTER

BARONESS SAYEEDA WARSI

THE RT REVD DR GULI FRANCIS-DEHQANI

DR ROWAN WILLIAMS

ZARA MOHAMMED

RABBI DAVID ROSEN KSG CBE

CARDINAL CORMAC MURPHY-O'CONNOR

RICHARD REED

CLAIRE WILLIAMS OBE

DAME STEPHANIE SHIRLEY

JULIE BENTLEY

DAVE FISHWICK

DR SARAH HUGHES

RICHARD FARLEIGH

MARVIN REES OBE

JACK KORNFIELD

Political, Religious & Business Leaders

SIR JOHN MAJOR
KG CH

SIR JOHN MAJOR served as prime minister of the United Kingdom and leader of the Conservative Party from 1990 to 1997. He previously held Cabinet positions under Prime Minister Margaret Thatcher, including foreign secretary and Chancellor of the Exchequer. Major was knighted by Queen Elizabeth II in 2005 for services to politics and charity, and was made a Member of the Order of the Companions of Honour in 1999 for his work on the Northern Ireland peace process.

FROM THE CHIEF OF STAFF

4 February, 2016

[handwritten salutation]

On behalf of Sir John I am replying to your recent letter, and do apologise for the delay in doing so.

You asked Sir John what he believed to be "the meaning of life", and the following is his response:

> *It is not easy to respond to this, except perhaps in the negative: life would have no meaning without family and friends, nor without an incentive for getting out of bed each morning. I could not be happy if I were idle, nor if the only things that motivated me were purely mercenary, with no personal interest or connection. We all need a purpose – large or small – and that, to me, is what gives life its meaning.*

I do hope this is helpful.

With all good wishes,

[signature]

ARABELLA WARBURTON

Mr James Bailey

IT IS NOT EASY TO RESPOND to this, except perhaps in the negative: life would have no meaning without family and friends, nor without an incentive for getting out of bed each morning. I could not be happy if I were idle, nor if the only things that motivated me were purely mercenary, with no personal interest or connection. We all need a purpose – large or small – and that, to me, is what gives life meaning.

'I could not be
happy if I
were idle.'

President
JIMMY CARTER

PRESIDENT JIMMY CARTER (1924–2024) served as the 39th president of the United States from 1977 to 1981. A member of the Democratic Party, Carter was the 76th governor of Georgia from 1971 to 1975, and a Georgia State senator from 1963 to 1967. After leaving the presidency, Carter established the Carter Center to promote and expand human rights, earning him a Nobel Peace Prize in 2002.

JAMES: OUR CREATOR GAVE US BOTH LIFE and freedom to
make our own decisions. We should strive to follow the perfect example
set by Jesus Christ.

Best wishes, Jimmy C

Baroness
SAYEEDA WARSI

BARONESS SAYEEDA WARSI is a lawyer, politician and member of the House of Lords who served as co-chairwoman of the Conservative Party from 2010 to 2012. She was appointed by Prime Minister David Cameron, in 2010, as minister without portfolio, becoming the first Muslim to serve as a Cabinet Minister. She also served as senior minister of state for the Foreign and Commonwealth Office and as the minister of state for Faith and Communities. She has been a racial justice campaigner for many years and was instrumental in the launch of Operation Black Vote, a not-for-profit national organisation that works towards greater racial justice and equality throughout the UK.

THE MEANING OF LIFE IS to find purpose and to live life purposefully.

A purposeful life I believe provides a reason for life, it provides structure, a meaning to getting up everyday and embracing the day. It provides, for me, a sense of mental and physical wellbeing and direction. It's a feeling of energy and when utilised it leaves me more energised not tired.

Many religions and cultures across the globe have embedded purpose into their teachings. From the concept of ikigai in Japanese culture, which focuses on living life in a way that is worthwhile and the feeling that drives willingness, to Ubuntu, an African philosophy and values system that suggests an interdependence of humans on one another and the acknowledgement of one's responsibility to their fellow humans and the world around them.

Islam, my faith, too defines purpose as service of God and service of mankind. The two are interconnected, fulfilling the latter allows us to live out our obligation to the former.

My purpose is a belief that each of us are custodians for a period of time in a place. We are custodians of our environment, our institutions, of our language and culture, of our communities and families.

For me the meaning of life is how we understand, acknowledge and try and fulfil our role as custodians.

Purpose is working out our strengths and utilising them in the place you act as a custodian.

For me this can be the ritual of my weekly litter pick or keeping the language of politics honest or speaking truth to power when it seeks to corrupt fundamental principles of democracy and the rule of law.

What can feel like difficult and brave public positions to take are far easier to take when they become a purpose. Not a singular moment but an overarching approach to life.

This may feel to others as a serious life, maybe even a life lacking fun and joy, and yet for me this approach to life is soulful and allows me to tread lightly through life. It feels like an easy way to live.

Without purpose for me life feels lost and directionless. It lacks the why behind what we do everyday. Purpose gives meaning to the small actions we make and gives structure to our time on this Earth. It makes me feel fulfilled, content and at peace.

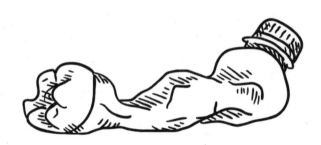

'We are custodians of our environment, our institutions, of our language and culture, of our communities and families.'

The Rt Revd Dr GULI FRANCIS-DEHQANI

DR GULI FRANCIS-DEHQANI is an Anglican bishop who has been bishop of Chelmsford since 2021. She was born in Iran, but when she was fourteen, her family was forced to leave the country in the wake of the Iranian Revolution. They settled in England, where Dr Guli studied music as an undergraduate, worked at the BBC, and then was ordained in 1998. She served as the first bishop of Loughborough, the suffragan bishop in the Diocese of Leicester from 2017 to 2021. She also serves as the Church of England's first bishop for housing and sits in Parliament as a Lord Spiritual.

I'M GRATEFUL FOR THE OPPORTUNITY to ponder these questions. The pace and demands of life mean that, without intentionality, there is often too little space to press pause and reflect. I know all too well what I do and usually how I do it, but it's good to wonder more about the mysteries that lie beneath the why – in other words the meaning behind it all. I write this in the week after Easter 2024, during a few days off. I suspect, at a different time and on a different day, my musings might have looked different. Moreover, in response to the vastness of the question, what I write feels inadequate – almost like a series of disjointed thoughts. I offer it in all humility as a small voice into the mix.

One of my children is currently an undergraduate studying philosophy. I told him I'd been invited to write on the meaning of life and asked him what he thought. *The first thing I'd do*, he said, *is interrogate what is meant by life. Is it all life, or your life?*

That seems as good a place as any to begin. So, what of all life? As a Christian and therefore a believer in a greater power, beyond the things we can see, know and understand, my instinct (which is honed by faith) is that God created life out of a desire to share the essence of God's self which is love. So, creation (or life) is an act of love – a longing for the selfless love that is shared in the relationship between the three persons of the Trinity (Father, Son and Holy Spirit) to move outwards and beyond the divine self.

And because the universe is a living thing, full of living beings – in other words full of life – it is also unpredictable and volatile. Life brings with it love and joy, freedom and fruitfulness, the potential for all that is good; but by its very nature, it also brings pain, failure, choices and even death. Life is a constant cycle of endings and new beginnings and we are invited to enter the mysterious rhythms of the sometimes aching realities we inhabit – to know that there is no love without pain, no life without death, no such thing as the individual without community. We can only taste the sweetness of love if we open ourselves to the possibility of pain. Indeed, that is the message of the Christian faith: a seed dying to bring new life, death leading to resurrection, love involving pain and sacrifice. Life and death are intertwined and life is all the sweeter because it lasts only for a season.

Jesus said, 'I came that they may have life, and have it abundantly' (John 10. 10). This implies that there's life, and then there's *life*. You might *exist* without experiencing the essence of life. The will to survive is fiercely strong and many overcome extraordinary suffering and hardship whilst clinging on to the desire to stay alive. The hope of better things to come is powerfully dynamic; the will to live, a formidable force. My mother, frail and weak in the latter stages of her life, lasted many days longer than the medics predicted. She was tenacious and determined in how she lived and, as she approached death, though there was no way back, the life force within her would not let go without a struggle.

So the instinct to survive is powerfully strong but what of life in all its abundant fullness – the life that Jesus spoke of in John chapter 10? This kind of life implies a sumptuous richness that includes a sense of meaning and purpose, blessings and the ability to navigate the ups and downs well; and brings me to the second part of my musings and a personal reflection on my own life and how I find meaning.

It is impossible to know *the* meaning of my life for sure. The best I can do is lean into the question, explore the many meanings I decipher and make the most of the time I have – try to make a difference (however small) for good. Even if you're of the view that creation came about through an infinite series of hollow coincidences, it still seems important to engage, at the very least, with the question of what things give meaning to your life and make it worth living. The meanings of my life are a complex blend that include the following ingredients.

Relationships – I have a need for them and a desire to cultivate them; with loved ones, friends, family, colleagues, passing acquaintances, chance encounters; and with God. I strive (and sometimes fail) towards reconciliation and forgiveness wherever possible, overcoming guilt, fear and regret – refusing to dwell on the things that damage and break down, in an effort to make better connections, learn and understand more deeply, about myself and others. As human beings we are reliant on God and one another. To acknowledge my need for connectedness through a range of relationships is to surrender the illusion of control and self-reliance. The need to love and be loved gives meaning to my life.

Sense of purpose – the opportunity to contribute and try to make a difference for good. I arrived in this country in 1980 as a refugee aged fourteen. I've reflected often on the need for asylum seekers and refugees to find a warm and dignified welcome if they are to be successful in making a new life. But along with welcome there is a deep need to contribute to their new society – to work, to volunteer, to use skills and experience. For me, this has included a desire to follow faithfully a sense of calling and vocation, to be a mother, to be a priest and bishop, a wife, a friend and many other things. Being able to find a sense of purpose in the opportunities life has afforded me provides fulfilment and meaning.

Identity and belonging – to make peace with who I am and to know that I'm loved and that I belong. My parents gave me the gift of unconditional love for which I feel blessed and give thanks daily. I was baptised as a baby and given my identity in Christ which supersedes all my other identities. And yet, for years I struggled with a sense of not belonging; both in Iran where I was born and grew up and where, by virtue of our faith as Christians we were regarded as 'foreigners', and also in this country where there was, for a long time, an uneasy sense of being an outsider who didn't quite fit in. But I have come to understand that many people feel this way for all kinds of different reasons. None of us fit neatly into a box but we are made up of a range of experiences and influences that shape who we are. I've tried to make peace with all that has made me who I am: the good, the bad and the ugly – without feeling trapped or constrained by it. I now understand that though I will never change the past there is always scope for transformation and new possibilities in the future. That is both comforting and provides impetus to continue pursuing a search for meaning.

One last thought, and it's about truth. Many people connect the search for meaning with the search for truth. However, the older I get, the more I feel that the search itself – the journey towards truth – is as important as the truth itself. Indeed, how we are with one another is in itself an expression of the most profound truth of what it means to be alive. Ultimately, perhaps it is not so much about trying to find meaning somewhere else, but rather having the courage to bring it into existence and embody it ourselves.

So, the meanings of life, in brief, and as I understand them.

Life in creation is an expression of God's love.

We and the whole of creation are interconnected. We need one another and God. We are to be good stewards of the world that has been entrusted to us, demonstrating love and respect towards one another.

To love, be in relationship and experience life in all its fullness is to feel pain and loss. We cannot understand or experience one without the other.

Our time on this earth is short, and kindness is an underrated value which underpins the meanings of life. We should use our time well and seek to make a difference for good. When we allow it, it's surprising how much good can come even out of bad situations.

Perhaps the meaning of life is to be found in trying to mirror in this life all that we hope for in the next.

Guli Francis-Dehqani
Bishop of Chelmsford
Easter Week 2024

'Life brings with it love and joy, freedom and fruitfulness, the potential for all that is good; but by its very nature, it also brings pain, failure, choices and even death.'

Dr ROWAN WILLIAMS

DR ROWAN WILLIAMS, Baron Williams of Oystermouth, is an Anglican bishop, theologian and poet. He was the 104th archbishop of Canterbury, a position he held from December 2002 to December 2012. Previously the bishop of Monmouth and archbishop of Wales, Dr Williams was the first archbishop of Canterbury in modern times not to be appointed from within the Church of England. After standing down as archbishop, he took up the position of chancellor of the University of South Wales in 2014 and served as master of Magdalene College, Cambridge between 2013 and 2020.

19 October 2015

Dear James,

Thank you for your letter and enquiry. It's never easy to answer the question of what is most meaningful to oneself, but I'd approach it along these lines:

As a Christian, I believe that life has its meaning from the gift of God. That is, life exists (all kinds of life) to show something of the beauty of God, and – in the case of intelligent life – to show something of God's overflowing selfless love. We are made in order to be vehicles of that love and to find joy in our sharing of it. Our worth and value therefore don't come from achievement but from this universal natural gift of dignity, a dignity reflecting God's intelligence and love. Honouring that in every person is the keystone of morality. And recognising that each of us is in need of love is the beginning of practical wisdom and humility. The next step is discovering how to be still and centred enough to receive love when it's given, instead of being chaotically anxious and aggressive and hyperactive, as our society encourages us to be. The story – and the living reality – of Jesus assures us that we are already embraced by God and that our salvation lies in believing that we are absolved and accepted and do not have to struggle to make ourselves loved by God. And this recognition transforms all our behaviour over time, so that greed and selfishness begin to fall away.

This is a very brief statement of what is central to my faith, but perhaps it will spark some thoughts for you!

Yours ever,

Rowan Williams

THANK YOU FOR YOUR LETTER AND ENQUIRY. It's never easy to answer the question of what is most meaningful to oneself, but I'd approach it along these lines:

As a Christian, I believe that life has its meaning from the gift of God. That is, life exists (all kinds of life) to show something of the beauty of God, and – in the case of intelligent life – to show something of God's overflowing selfless love. We are made in order to be vehicles of that love to find joy in our sharing of it. Our worth and value therefore don't come from achievement but from this universal natural gift of dignity, a dignity reflecting God's intelligence and love. Honouring that in every person is the keystone of morality. And recognizing that each of us is in need of love is the beginning of practical wisdom and humility. The next step is discovering how to be still and centred enough to receive love when it's given, instead of being chaotically anxious and aggressive and hyperactive, as our society encourages us to be. The story – and the living reality – of Jesus assures us that we are already embraced by God and that our salvation lies in believing that we are absolved and accepted and do not have to struggle to make ourselves loved by God. And this recognition transforms all our behaviour over time, so that greed and selfishness begin to fall away.

This is a very brief statement of what is central to my faith, but perhaps it will spark some thoughts for you.

Yours ever,

Rowan Williams

'Our worth and value don't come from achievement.'

ZARA
MOHAMMED

ZARA MOHAMMED is the secretary general of the Muslim Council of Britain. She is the first woman to lead the organisation. The Muslim Council of Britain is a national umbrella body with over 500 mosques and educational and charitable associations affiliated to it. It includes national, regional, local and specialist Muslim organisations and institutions from different ethnic and sectarian backgrounds within major parts of, but not all, British Islamic society. When appointed, Mohammed additionally became the youngest, as well as the first Scottish, person to serve in the role.

I'M A MUSLIM, I BELIEVE IN GOD and the hereafter, but for me, the greatest act of worship to serve God is to serve humanity. I don't see that as just serving my community and Muslims, that just happens to be the space I'm in. I feel helping people is my ultimate calling, and it was how I was brought up. My dad's a chef, and he once told me a story of someone coming in to the restaurant who was hungry but didn't have any money. My dad simply told him to sit down and fed him. Whilst we may have our own faiths and beliefs, we're all part of a global family and we should try to take care of everyone.

I was born and raised in Glasgow. I'm third-generation Pakistani Scottish. And I think finding myself has been one of my biggest challenges. I still remember in primary school when the teacher asked us all to draw ourselves. Everybody else drew an assortment of stick-related human beings. I was the only one to draw myself like a superhero with different colour hair and a cape and flying ability. I always remember that because I never felt as if I really fitted in with everybody else, at least not until university where I was able to find myself a bit more.

There I joined different societies and clubs, and actually ended up running for the Student Union President – mainly because I spent so much time in the Union! It was in the second year of university when I decided to put my headscarf on. Before that I was a practising Muslim, but I wasn't overtly Muslim. I was already praying and reading, but wearing the headscarf strengthened my faith, in part because of everybody else's reaction to it. It's a global symbol with certain connotations, and I felt more conscious that people become uncomfortable with me – whether that was at university or on public transport or in the street. In some ways this made me really decide who I wanted to be. Because if I wanted to take this identity, or if I wanted this to be part of me, which it is now, then I had to have the resolve and the strength to wear it.

According to the Quran, your purpose in life is to worship God – we pray five times a day – but God doesn't assess what you do. Rather it's all about your intentions and efforts for doing it. It's about serving God, serving humanity, taking care of the earth, taking care of the spiritual wellness of the Muslim community, but also it's about emboldening values like justice, righteousness, love and compassion.

I think it's really important to live your purpose. I always felt like I wanted to help in the community space. After university, I became involved in the Muslim Council of Britain (MCB) but I was tired of the way some communities are treated or perceived by the media, and I didn't feel I was being served well by my representatives. Someone suggested that I ran in the MCB election. Of course, I thought who is going to vote for me? A twenty-eight-year-old from Glasgow, the first woman . . . I just thought they were totally bananas.

The minute I was elected as Secretary General of the Muslim Council of Britain in 2021, my whole life changed and I became a public figure. I was suddenly in the national papers and international media. I was even featured in *Vogue*! It was crazy. But I didn't sign up to become a famous person, I wanted to serve British Muslim communities. I wanted to be a positive contributing force to Britain, and to young people.

It can be hard work as I'm trying to serve my community, but also ripping apart the old ways of doing things. I'm the youngest person in the organisation, but also the boss. Fifty per cent of Muslims in this country are under twenty-five years old so a huge amount of my demographic are young people who are counting on me, and the MCB has provided me a vehicle to be a different kind of voice. I realised that even the *Vogue* feature meant a lot to the girls and women in my community because I was being normalised. I received messages from mums saying you don't know how much that means for my fourteen-year-old to see you there. Another girl said, I really struggle with my headscarf, and you've just given me so much confidence.

I certainly don't want to regret having had this amazing opportunity so I'm constantly thinking what is the maximum good that I can do? But I do believe it's not so much about what you achieve, but who you become in the process of that achievement. I could achieve everything as Secretary General, but if I don't become a very nice person, if I lose myself in the process, I don't know if that's necessarily a win. The more good I can do, the more I can serve people, the more I can help – that's what makes me feel like I've achieved something. And also by taking the risk in doing things that no one's ever done before and putting yourself in the scariest places you can imagine, you're also creating a path for other people to follow.

It's clear that we're all looking for a sense of purpose, and Islam provides that for me. Others may find that purpose in serving their family or their loved ones. But for those more spiritually inclined to Islam, what I've found is that there's a path that we're following to get closer to God. Through your acts of worship, you get closer to God. And as you get closer to God, you find peace in your heart. Because ultimately, our souls were always with God in the first place. And then no matter what happens – whether you're in poverty or a war zone – there's comfort from knowing that you have your Creator with you.

Rabbi DAVID ROSEN
KSG CBE

RABBI DAVID ROSEN is the former chief rabbi of Ireland, the American Jewish Committee's International director of interreligious affairs and special advisor to the Abrahamic Family House in Abu Dhabi. He is an international president of the Religions for Peace and served for ten years on the Board of Directors of the King Abdullah International Center for Interreligious and Intercultural Dialogue. In 2005, the Pope made Rabbi Rosen a Knight Commander of the Order of St Gregory the Great in recognition of his contribution to Catholic–Jewish reconciliation; and in 2010 he was named a Commander of the British Empire by Queen Elizabeth II for his interreligious work.

UNDERSTANDING 'THE MEANING OF LIFE' to mean the purpose of life, my reply would be that the meaning of life is in giving life meaning.

There are different ways in which we can do that, above all through awareness and appreciation (what is often called mindfulness in the West today, under new-found Dharma influences). I would argue that the whole of Judaism as a religious way of life is designed to instil such awareness, mindfulness, in all we do. But perhaps what epitomizes this is the concept of a brachah, a blessing. Jewish teaching requires that we make a blessing before enjoying any physical benefit (as well as for any special occasion), most obviously before eating or drinking, and there are traditional formulae for this. Thus, for example, before an observant Jew eats an apple, he pauses for a moment and recites the formula, 'Blessed are you O Lord our God, Sovereign of the Universe who creates the fruit of the tree.' In so doing, we raise our consciousness and gratitude to the Creator for the pleasure and benefit we are about to derive, so that the most basic of human needs is not simply an instinctive automatic physical reaction. Thus, something as basic as eating acquires spiritual meaning. This idea should animate our relationship with the whole natural world and acquires its greatest importance in our relations with other human beings – all 'created in the Divine Image', so that we are conscious and aware as much as possible of the fact that every human encounter is an encounter with the Divine to some extent, even with those whose actions appear to deny that very premise.

The extent to which we nourish relationships (above all with other people, but also with other sentient beings and with the natural environment as a whole), increasing responsibility, respect, and love in the world – especially through caring for the vulnerable and the needy, seeking to alleviate suffering and pain – the more we give meaning to our own lives, and the more we actually increase the very meaning of life.

I could go on in this regard, but hope that the above is of value.

In case your question indicates a desire to know the 'intention' of the Creator, I would say that that question is no more valid than why does an artist paint. The painting is who (what) the artist is! Life, i.e. the Creation, is simply the manifestation of the Divine presence and power (and potential), and religions seek to understand the ethical nature of that power so that humanity may live by and according to that knowledge.

My best wishes and regards from Jerusalem.

David

'Jewish teaching requires that we make a blessing before enjoying any physical benefit … Thus, something as basic as eating acquires spiritual meaning.'

Cardinal CORMAC MURPHY-O'CONNOR

CARDINAL CORMAC MURPHY-O'CONNOR (1932–2017) was the former archbishop of Westminster and president of the Catholic Bishops' Conference of England and Wales. He was made cardinal by Pope John Paul II in 2001.

Dear James,

Thank you for your letter. There is a lot one can say but can I limit it?

Life's meaning for me is under the Providence of God. I said a prayer this morning, 'Here I am Lord, I come to do your will'. So I find my happiness in serving other people, loving other people, seeing in them some image, however faint, of the love of God.

I am sorry this reply is so short. I will say a special prayer for you.

With my kind wishes,

Yours devotedly,

+Cormac Card. Murphy-O'Connor
Archbishop Emeritus of Westminster

THANK YOU FOR YOUR LETTER. There is a lot one can say but can I limit it?

Life's meaning for me is under the Providence of God. I said a prayer this morning, 'Here I am Lord, I come to do your will.' So I find my happiness in serving other people, loving other people, seeing in them some image, however faint, of the love of God.

I am sorry this reply is so short. I will say a special prayer for you.

With my kind wishes,

Yours devotedly,

+Cormac Card. Murphy-O'Connor

Archbishop Emeritus of Westminster

RICHARD REED

RICHARD REED is the co-founder of Innocent Drinks, the UK and Europe's number-one smoothie brand. In 1999, Reed and two university friends started selling smoothies at music festivals and transformed their idea into a business with a turnover of £200 million. The company gives 10 per cent of its profits to charity, and funds a separate charity called the Innocent Foundation that invests in rural development in the countries where the fruit comes from. After selling their controlling stake to Coca-Cola, Reed launched Jam Jar Investments to help fund a new wave of entrepreneurs. Reed has also served as a non-executive director on the Department of Energy and Climate Change, sat on the Development Board of Oxfam and acted as a government adviser on entrepreneurship.

TO SEARCH FOR THE MEANING of life belittles it.

Life is the point.

The unrepeatable, impossibly unlikely gift that countless unlucky billions throughout eternity never received.

It is not about whether your glass is half full or half empty, it is about realising that you have a glass.

But we often ask why have we been given a life?

That answer is simple: to help each other.

And how to enrich it?

By doing what we can each day, to deepen the quality of relationships we have with the family and friends around us, sometimes including the ones we haven't met yet.

Dancing and surfing helps too.

'Life is the point.'

CLAIRE
WILLIAMS OBE

CLAIRE WILLIAMS is the former deputy team principal of the Williams Formula 1 racing team and one of only two women to have ever managed a Formula 1 team in the modern era. Under her leadership, Williams finished 3rd in the World Championship for Constructors in 2014 and 2015. During her tenure, Williams was a keen advocate for greater diversity and inclusion within Williams Racing and across the sport as a whole. As vice president of the Spinal Injuries Association, Williams also sought to encourage spinal cord-injured individuals into the team and established workplace opportunities for wheelchair users. In April 2023 she launched the Sir Frank Williams Academy, which aims to provide life-changing care for spinal cord-injured people.

I WAS IN THE GARAGE ONE RACE WEEKEND with my dad, just quietly alongside each other after qualifying, when he turned to me and said, 'Aren't we just the luckiest people alive, Claire? We get to do this. Everyday. And we get paid for it. There is no greater privilege.'

Those words stayed with me my whole career. Through the good times and the bad. And they stay with me today. Because life is short, because it's hard so much of the time; to find something you love to do is, for me, the key to finding happiness, balance and peace in life.

'To find something you love to do is, for me, the key to finding happiness, balance and peace in life.'

Dame STEPHANIE SHIRLEY CH

DAME STEPHANIE (STEVE) SHIRLEY is an ardent venture philanthropist with an unrelenting energy for creating positive change. She arrived in England as an unaccompanied child refugee at the start of the Second World War. In 1962, she started a software business from her dining table which grew to employ 8,500 people. As an all-woman software company, it pioneered remote working and redefined the expectations and opportunities for working women at the time. It was ultimately valued at almost $3 billion and made seventy of her staff millionaires. Since 'retiring', her work has been in philanthropy, with a particular focus on autism and IT. She has given away more than £67 million of her personal wealth to different projects.

I HOPE YOU ARE WELL AND THANK YOU for setting such a profound challenge. I share with the great Rousseau the belief that 'the meaning of life is a life of meaning'.

For so it has been for me. I love to learn. And life is more fulfilling if you can see beyond yourself, if you can understand the broader picture. That means having goals for your community, your profession and your country. Country is crucial to me as I was an unaccompanied child refugee who reached sanctuary in Britain in 1939.

I took my maths degree while working as a sort of mathematical clerk at a leading research institute. There I worked on early computers and revelled in the intellectual ambience, while resenting the sexism of the times.

This led in 1962 to my founding Freelance Programmers to write tailor-made computer software using women with domestic responsibilities working from home. The next four decades were full of trials and tribulations, passion and pleasure.

It was a slow burn; but after twenty-five years the company paid its first dividend and thereafter was a commercial success. I took the company into co-ownership – the most costly gift of my life.

As then an ardent philanthropist, I found the simple truth: the wealth which creates the greatest pleasure is the wealth you give away. I set up three autism charities and took them to independence. My interest in computers and gender-related topics remains but the focus of my life has now turned to autism, my late son's condition.

My fulfilment stems from my personal growth and passion for humanity's wellbeing. At four score and ten, I have done what was in me to do.

Sincerely yours

Dame Stephanie Shirley CH

JULIE BENTLEY

JULIE BENTLEY is a UK voluntary sector leader and chief executive officer of Samaritans. She has been a charity CEO for over twenty years and has led some of the UK's most well-known charity names, including Action for Children, Girlguiding, Family Planning Association and the Suzy Lamplugh Trust. She has been included in the top ten of Britain's most influential women in the BBC Woman's Hour Power List, named the 'Most Admired Charity CEO', and has been castaway on BBC Radio 4's *Desert Island Discs*.

I DON'T SPEND MUCH TIME WONDERING why I'm on this earth; I have a pretty straightforward view on that. I'm here as a consequence of a pregnancy that resulted in my birth! None of us choose to be born, but here we are and generally none of us know how long or how little time we have of this thing called life.

For me, the meaning of life is about purpose, and I have spent a lot of time thinking about how to spend my time.

I am a humanist. A humanist is someone who is non-religious. As a humanist, I believe there is only one life and so I need to make the most of it. For humanists, there is no single 'ultimate' meaning of life. Instead, it is up to us to make our own lives meaningful, for me that is about anchoring my view of the world in science and reason and focusing on human connection in the here and now.

I have brought meaning and purpose to my life through seeking to embrace as much as possible of the wonderful world we are privileged to inhabit. To visit different countries, experience many cultures and be open to difference and diversity. To spend time in nature, appreciating how extraordinary, beautiful, and sadly vulnerable the natural world is.

A large part of the meaning in my life has come from my career in the charity sector. For me having the opportunity to work across a range of issues that impact individuals and society such as poverty, homelessness, addiction, sexual and reproductive rights, young people's wellbeing and mental health has afforded me a deep understanding of the very different lives people have and immersed me in the myriad real challenges people face.

323

But also, because of dedicating my career to the charity sector, I have witnessed so much good too, working alongside people who want to make a positive impact on their community, wider society and the world.

I have sought to bring meaning to my life through a balance of immersing myself in and celebrating this one short life, building, and cherishing the rich relationship I have with others, alongside being committed to serve our wider society and indeed the world as a global citizen.

I try to play my small part in increasing happiness, hope, equity, and opportunity for all people and to act in ways that reduce or challenge inequity, discrimination, and injustice. Because alongside squeezing every drop of life out of this one I have for myself, it also brings meaning to my life to feel I am supporting and accompanying others on their journeys too.

Humans are connected in ways that are obvious and in far more ways it can be harder to recognise. Deep and wide-reaching human connection is central to my life meaning and is also the source of much happiness to me.

'As a humanist, I believe there is only one life and so I need to make the most of it.'

DAVE FISHWICK

DAVE FISHWICK is an entrepreneur, businessman and philanthropist. In 2011, he founded Burnley Savings and Loans Ltd, championing UK banking reform with his firm belief that ordinary working people should have access to specific financial products and services. His mission was documented in Channel 4's 2012 hit show *Bank of Dave*. He has gone on to appear in a number of other documentary series, and is a two-time BAFTA winner, a *Sunday Times* best-selling author and the subject of the 2023 Netflix movie *The Bank of Dave*.

I LEFT SCHOOL WITH ABSOLUTELY NOTHING. I had no qualifications and no skills. I went straight to work on a building site as a builder's labourer. How did I go from being a builder's labourer to building the first new high street bank in over 150 years in Britain? If I can do it, a lad from Burnley with no qualifications, then anybody can.

I see many influencers on social media spraying expensive bottles of champagne into the sea, telling kids you don't have to work to become wealthy and prosperous; however, let me be very clear: there is no easy way to become rich and successful. I had three jobs, and the secret to success is hard work, and hard work will put you where some good luck can find you!

You need to invest in yourself and learn to communicate better; communication skills are critical in writing and in person, increasing your net worth by at least 50 per cent. You have to be able to put forward your ideas. If you invest in yourself, nobody can ever take that away. Invest in learning skills; whatever the skill, you can always sell that skill, and it will be inflation-proof and abilities can never be taken away from you. For instance, if you are the best teacher, lawyer, surgeon or plumber, you can be inflation-proof because the price of your skills will always increase with inflation. It does work.

Stress will come in life and in business, but you must understand that stress doesn't come from hard work. Stress primarily comes from not taking action on something you have some control over, so when the stress arrives, take action as soon as possible, and the stress starts dissipating quickly.

If it's a good idea, just do it in life. It's far easier to apologise after than it is to get permission in the beginning and in life, everyone will keep telling you you have no chance, but you must learn to turn No's into Yes's! Remember, a Yes is a Yes, a maybe is a Yes, and a No is just a delayed Yes!

It's okay to go to bed at night, saying to yourself, I've made a mistake today, but remember to tell yourself that I will definitely not make that same mistake again tomorrow. If you don't make mistakes, then you're not trying hard enough.

Surround yourself with good people, and good things will happen. Try to find people who are better than you, and you will go in that direction, I promise.

The secret to a happy life is not to have much envy and resentment. Don't overspend your income. Envy is one of the deadly sins that you will never have any fun with. Stay cheerful despite your troubles, and surround yourself with good, honest, reliable, ethical people. Good things will happen.

Self-belief and common sense are everything. Nobody else will believe in you if you don't believe in yourself. Self-belief allows you to make anything possible.

You must adapt, adjust and overcome all problems; the most important two rules in life are rule number one, never give up, and rule number two, never ever give up!

Win it fairly and use it wisely, which will set you on the right path. Good luck.

'The secret to a happy life is not to have much envy and resentment.'

Dr SARAH HUGHES

DR SARAH HUGHES is the chief executive officer of Mind, the UK's leading mental health charity. She has worked in mental health and criminal justice for thirty-five years. After originally training as a social worker, Hughes has spent the majority of her career in the voluntary sector within both community and secure settings. She holds advisory and board roles with organisations including the FA, Kooth PLC and IIMHL, is a fellow of the Royal Society of Arts, Sciana and Salzburg Global. She is also a social commentator and has been invited to speak at many international events. In 2022 she achieved her professional doctorate studying women and leadership.

I'M KNOWN THEREFORE I AM ...

I was taught about Descartes and other philosophers when I was 16. The otherworldly ideas blew my teenage mind. These lessons encouraged me to daydream, expand my world view and question everything. It was a Pandora's box moment. I think that was the first conscious time I asked myself the existential question, what is the meaning of life?

Before I go on, there is a caveat. I've had a couple of tries during my life at working out the meaning of life, but one thing that I keep coming back to is that the answer can't be just one thing. Our lives are so complex and unpredictable that I don't buy the single meaning theory, the universe doesn't design simply. I think there is a basic tier subscription to meaning and then we build on top of that by the very virtue of our humanity. The universality of love has to be the bottom line for us all, surely! I know, cliché, sorry, but to love and to be loved is the magic of life, the joy and sorrow, the space for true connection and intimacy. I don't just mean erotic love, I'm talking all love, familial, the love of your cat, your best girlfriend. Love, in my view, foregrounds everything else.

I went to a Catholic Convent grammar school for girls during the 80s/90s, the nuns were from the Servite Sisters, a religious order who believed the meaning of life was service to God and communities. They became nurses, teachers and missionaries. My parents also had that deep sense of service and I regularly accompanied them on matters of community, taking food to neighbours, organising local events, volunteering. It made sense for me to follow their lead so I joined the social sector and as a result have worked for charities for more than 35 years. But, as I've learned and evolved over the years, the concept of service is not quite right. It belies the truth of ego, altruism and status: it's a red herring. It also carries connotations of saviourism that didn't align with my belief in the power of others.

This led me to the second version of my truth, I hypothesised that if my sense of service is powered by social injustice, then maybe my meaning is one of honour and integrity. I was almost born wearing a beret and Doctor Martens, I remember my first feminist rant at the age of 4 with my grandad, it was about women drivers! I call these my 'missionary years', meaning it was all a bit sacrificial and martyrish, full of virtue signalling and blunder. I was perched on the moral high ground, powered by the beguiling narrative that I was a 'good person'. But, this soon felt artificial and exhausting, and didn't allow for my mistakes. It couldn't last.

Now I'm approaching 50, my thinking has evolved again. I think that the meaning of life is to be known, seen, heard, and understood. The most pain I've seen in my life personally and professionally has been caused by not being accepted for being your true self. Sometimes of course the choice about whether we can be authentic or not is subject to scrutiny, systemic barriers and judgement from others, an injustice in and of itself. But, by focusing on authenticity rather than integrity I gave myself the psychological space for curiosity and learning, and ultimately getting it wrong. By being authentic I can still be taught new things, I can engage people on an equal footing. I recognise my strengths and play to them, keep vigilance on my weaknesses with hopeful commitment to doing better. Honour and integrity are part of it. The moral high ground is seductive but it's a false God and will leave you with nowhere to hide or evolve, and frankly people won't like or trust you.

In the end, it's only you who can decide what the meaning of your life is. All I know is that in a curious and just world there is space for us all.

'I think that the meaning of life is to be known, seen, heard, and understood.'

RICHARD FARLEIGH

RICHARD FARLEIGH is one of the UK's most renowned angel investors and serial entrepreneurs, and a former Dragon on BBC's *Dragons' Den*. Despite being born into an impoverished family who lived in a tent in the Australian outback, Farleigh managed to overcome all odds and forge himself a hugely successful career in finance. He has invested in more than eighty start-ups in the UK, of which a substantial number have become their own success stories. He has also served as chancellor of the London South Bank University and is an internationally ranked chess player.

AS I GET OLDER, memories fade but their meanings clarify
I've been through a children's shelter and the fostering system
I've been poor and very lonely
And I've been lucky

I've been educated and found a career
I've met many strangers
I've been religious and I've studied math
I've read a lot
I've been generous and fought my flaws

Looking back, it's been other people who made the difference
Their small acts or big acts of kindness
It's not just the outcomes, but the warmth
School teachers come to mind, and other special people
They are the hidden arrows between the shadows and the lights of the
photograph of my life

Good people. I pull them in close.
Whatever *is* the meaning of life,
we are finding out, together.

Best wishes, Rich

MARVIN
REES OBE

MARVIN REES is a British Labour Party politician and the first mayor of Black African heritage to lead a European city, serving as the mayor of Bristol from 2016 to 2024. During his eight-year tenure, he oversaw everything in the city through Brexit to Covid, the cost-of-living crisis to the fall of the Edward Colston statue. Rees is also a Yale World Fellow and co-founded the City Leadership Programme.

WHEN I WAS YOUNG I THOUGHT I believed in singular truths. That was partly a product of the way I engaged with and expressed the evangelical Christianity I was part of. I am not saying those kinds of truths don't exist but as I have got older I have become more aware that I actually sit most comfortably with truths that are multidimensional and mysterious.

That is how I reflected on this question about the meaning of life. I actually prefer to talk about meanings (plural), but I do think there is meaning. I think the mere fact that I can reflect on, or desire, a meaning suggests there is – not least because having considered it, giving up on meaning would leave me feeling less meaningful.

I think that the meanings of life are probably like mathematical laws – we discover them, name and describe them, and we make them, and there is a mysterious dance between all of that. So I would discover meaning in the act of searching, but that meaning only exists and is accessible because I am searching and know I am searching.

I am clearly not a philosopher so I thought it would be safest for me to reflect when I have found life most meaningful.

In 1990 I was in Spitzbergen with the British Exploring Society. I was sat on top of a mountain with three friends. Nobody had ever climbed that mountain before. We each faced different directions looking out across the hundreds of snow-covered mountain tops with the fjords, glacial lakes and glacial valleys running between them. At about 11:50pm we all shut up to ensure we would be silent as the midnight sun circled us. I looked down and below me was a huge crevasse. I thought to myself, 'If I fell down there, nobody would ever see my body again.' In all that, I became very aware of the smallness and fragility of my existence in the bigness of the world. And yet I was alive, and I was aware that I was alive, and that awareness was enormous. I found meaning in my insignificance.

My sister had accepted a place at university and was looking for accommodation. We had grown up without much money or a family car but my first job out of university provided me with a wage and a company car. It meant I was able to drive my sister to Southampton with no problem. We spent the day with agents looking for accommodation. We came to one we liked but the agent was being a bit non-committal. I leant in and loudly whispered, 'If you want this house, I'll write a check for £500 now.' The agent immediately changed tone and my sister had a secure home. I was only earning about £15k and the check was only £500 but I was able to provide for my sister and give a security we struggled to find growing up. I found meaning in the opportunity to put love into action.

In 2021, I was in the US visiting with my Jamaican family. My cousin shared that he had been tracing our ancestry and showed me a diagram he had drawn. It goes back to my great, great, great, great grandfather Samuel Richardson. Next to his name it says, 'HANGED – 1865. Morant Bay Rebellion.' I included this story in my October 2022 State of the City address. I had tried to imagine what was going through his mind as he stood on the gallows waiting to die. Was he afraid? Did he think this was it? Did he think his life had come to nothing? I got a bit choked up as I wondered if he could have imagined his great great great great grandson would become mayor of a city that was one of the UK's biggest slave ports and the first person of black African heritage to be elected mayor of any European city? I found meaning in giving his fight and his life and hopes meaning, and in discovering my connection to a bigger story.

I can't sign off without sharing that I do find meaning in a God. I can't fully define what I mean by God, but I would struggle to make sense of the purposeful language we have to use when we talk about people, planet or universe. And if there are purposes interacting all around us, I am not separate from them. And in them I will have an opportunity to find some meaning.

'I got a bit choked up as I wondered if he could have imagined his great great great great grandson would become mayor of a city that was one of the UK's biggest slave ports?'

JACK KORNFIELD

JACK KORNFIELD trained as a Buddhist monk in the monasteries of Thailand, India and Burma. He has taught meditation internationally since 1974 and is one of the key teachers to introduce Buddhist mindfulness practice to the West. His books have been translated into twenty languages and sold more than a million copies.

IN THE END 3 THINGS MATTER.
Did I love well?
Did I live fully?
Did I learn to let go?

OLIVER BURKEMAN

DR SARA KUBURIC

CELESTE HEADLEE

MARK MANSON

BETH KEMPTON

CORY ALLEN

PROFESSOR PETER ADAMSON

MELISSA STERRY

MARK STEVENSON

JOSHUA FLETCHER

GRETCHEN RUBIN

CHARLES DUHIGG

ROXIE NAFOUSI

MATT RIDLEY

ADAM GRANT

Thinkers, Philosophers & Futurists

OLIVER
BURKEMAN

OLIVER BURKEMAN is an author and journalist, whose books include *The Antidote: Happiness for People Who Can't Stand Positive Thinking, Help! How to Become Slightly Happier and Get a Bit More Done* and the best-selling *Four Thousand Weeks: Time Management for Mortals*, a self-help book on the philosophy and psychology of time management and happiness. For many years, he wrote a popular weekly column on psychology for the *Guardian*, 'This Column Will Change Your Life'. His work has also appeared in the *New York Times*, *Wall Street Journal*, *Psychologies* and *New Philosopher*.

I HOPE YOU WILL PARDON the brevity – your message suggests that you will.

I agree with the scholar of myth Joseph Campbell that it makes more sense to say that what we're seeking isn't a meaning for life, so much as the experience of feeling fully alive. There are experiences that I know, in my bones, are 'why I'm here' – unhurried time with my son, or deep conversations with my wife, hikes in the North York Moors, writing and communicating with people who've found liberation in something I have written. I would struggle, though, if I were to try to argue that any of these will 'mean something', in some kind of timeless way, for example five hundred years from now. What's changed for me is that I no longer feel that these experiences need this particular kind of justification. I want to show up fully, or as fully as possible, for my time on earth. That's all – but then again I think that is everything. And so I try, on a daily basis, to navigate more and more by that feeling of aliveness – rather than by the feeling of wanting to be in control of things, which is alluring, but deadening in the end.

Dr SARA KUBURIC

DR SARA KUBURIC is an existential psychotherapist, consultant, columnist for *USA Today* and the person behind the popular Instagram page @millennial.therapist. Her interest in psychology stems from her personal experience living through wars, navigating complex relationships and continually learning what it means to be human. She is passionate about helping people seek change and live authentic, free and meaningful lives.

MEANING IS AS ELUSIVE AS IT IS TANGIBLE. The question, 'What is the meaning of life?' is theoretical, yet the answer is embodied and visceral. We recognize meaning when we feel it, when it resonates within us.

Humans don't merely seek to know 'why' they are alive, we seek to experience the essence of living.

Sometimes, I think, we overcomplicate the search for meaning. What if it's not some grand revelation but rather found in the everyday moments? A result of countless decisions, experiences and behaviors that shape our lives – a simple conversation, a cup of tea, a tender kiss, or a scribble on a piece of paper. What if that's all there is to it?

What if meaning is just our ability to be present enough to feel the value of our existence?

I (personally) want to use life, play with it, and wear it out – like an old, comfortable pair of shoes. I want to participate and be moved, provoked and expanded by my very existence.

Every day, I strive to confront the possibility of meaninglessness head-on. I attempt to take responsibility for my actions and choices, recognizing that they dictate the course of my life and whether or not I will perceive it as meaningful. I pay attention to what makes me feel alive, what allows me to express myself, and what drains me of vitality.

Meaning emerges as a consequence of how I show up in the world and is guided by the constant dialogue between my Self and my life.

CELESTE
HEADLEE

CELESTE HEADLEE is a journalist, and the best-selling author of *We Need To Talk: How to Have Conversations That Matter*, *Do Nothing: How to Break Away from Overworking, Overdoing, and Underliving*, *Speaking of Race: Why Everyone Needs to Talk About Racism and How to Do It* and *You're Cute When You're Mad: Simple Steps for Confronting Sexism*. Her TEDx Talk, *10 Ways to Have a Better Conversation*, has been viewed over thirty-four million times.

THERE ARE SO FEW THINGS that I know about life and so little empirical evidence to support any claim I might make that life has any meaning at all. So much of what exists is the product of chaos and random chance, that it's hard to ascribe a deeper explanation for the continued existence of dolphins and button mushrooms and ladybugs, and humans.

As I've aged, I have come to realize that I don't have a purpose in life, so much as an opportunity to be purposeful. Now, in my fifth decade, I derive meaning from the moments that have made lasting impressions on me and on those around me, the decisions that impacted not just myself but also others, human or otherwise. Opting for a dessert that I enjoy doesn't seem particularly meaningful; it's enjoyed for a short span of time by only one person. But the tiny food pantry that my neighbors and I installed so that anyone who is hungry can get food, no questions asked, has been used by dozens of people who probably shared what they got with their families and friends. Perhaps having access to the pantry relieved their stress in a minor way, which also had ripple effects on their lives. And the experience of service, of being useful to others, has made me happier and more centered, which altered my mood and influenced the way I interact with others.

Those choices have meaning because their impact was not isolated and the consequences were generally positive.

Life is disordered and often painful.

The only reliable method I have for connecting with deeper significance is by making choices that are creative and not destructive, expansive and not self-centered, and kind instead of mercenary.

I create meaning by being useful to other living beings. I think that's all I can do.

MARK MANSON

MARK MANSON is the three-time #1 *New York Times* best-selling author of *The Subtle Art of Not Giving a F*ck*, as well as other titles. His books have sold twenty million copies, been translated into more than sixty-five languages, and reached number one in more than a dozen countries. In 2023, a feature film about his life and ideas was released worldwide by Universal Pictures.

LIFE HAS NO INHERENT MEANING.

I believe a sense of meaning is a byproduct of one's actions and relationships.

When I feel like I lack meaning in my life, I ask myself, 'If I were to die in a year, what would I feel an urgency to do?'

The answer to that question then becomes my compass.

'When I feel like I lack meaning in my life, I ask myself, "If I were to die in a year, what would I feel an urgency to do?"'

BETH KEMPTON

BETH KEMPTON is a Japanologist and the best-selling author of *Wabi Sabi: Japanese Wisdom for a Perfectly Imperfect Life* and *Kokoro: Japanese Wisdom for a Life Well Lived*. She is also a Reiki master trained in the Japanese tradition in Tokyo, a qualified yoga teacher and an award-winning entrepreneur and producer of online courses that have helped thousands of people to find personal, professional and financial freedom.

THE MEANING OF 'LIFE' IS, literally, to be alive. To experience the animation of breath and the growth that comes with constant change up until the moment of death. But of course when we ask this question of meaning we are asking 'What is the point?', to which 'breathing' is not a satisfactory answer, even if it is often a useful solution in any challenging life situation. In terms of the point of life as a human being I can't help thinking it is to sense and know our role in the web of everything, and contribute to that web in some way.

In recent years, as a kind of midlife malaise has collided with devastating loss in my life, I have thought deeply about what it means to have 'success' as a human. I have realised that I have carried a misbelief about 'success' for most of my life, and have only recently come to understand that actually success has nothing to do with your outer life and what other people think of you. Rather, it's about the richness of your inner life, and the way you show up in the world with love and consideration for others. It's about the joy, beauty and wonder that you find in the world, and how you share that through the way that you live.

I can't help but think that this is, in some way, connected to the meaning of life. Perhaps the meaning is the experience of being alive, the purpose is what we do with that experience as part of the wider ecosystem of life, past, present and future, and the point is to be awake to all of it, before it all vanishes, in full awareness that it will.

CORY ALLEN

CORY ALLEN is an author, podcast host and meditation teacher. On his podcast, *And Then It Hit Me,* he discusses how to live better through teachings on mindfulness, mental clarity and personal growth. Through his popular online meditation course *Release into Now,* he has helped thousands of people learn to meditate with clarity and simplicity. His first book, *Now Is the Way,* was published in 2019.

In conversation with the man Durant encountered who said he was going to kill himself unless he was given a valid reason not to:

The man requested,

'I'm going to take my own life unless you can show me a reason not to.'

I answered,

'Where have you looked for a reason so far? I don't want to waste what might turn out to be your precious time.'

The man said,

'I've thought as big as I can. Why are we here at all? Who created the universe? What's the point? I can't find an answer that really matters.'

I responded,

'Have you considered that if you can choose to die, you can also choose to live?

The man answered,

'Yes.'

I replied,

'So, have you tried living yet?'

The man replied,

'I've done what I was told I was supposed to do in life, and it hasn't made me happy.'

I answered,

'Ah, so you are alive but have yet to choose to live. See, most people confuse the meaning of life with meaning in life. The meaning of life is simple. It is to live. Unfortunately, people don't tend to look deeply at things. So being present in the abundance of existence isn't enough to make them happy. They need to fill their lives with a story of meaning to make it feel like this all counts.'

The man asked,

'How do I fill my life with meaning?'

I replied,

'Create it through your actions. You have to pay attention to what you do in life that makes you feel more alive – then do more of that. It doesn't matter if the thing you do is big or small, cool or corny, permanent or fleeting. Meaning isn't about what you do. It's about how what you do makes you feel.'

The man responded,

'So, if I do what makes me feel more alive, I'll create meaning in my life and be happy?'

I responded,

'Yes, because then you'll be living. The more time you spend doing what makes you feel alive, the more you will feel like you have purpose because the actions in your life have direction. After you feel like you have a purpose for a while, you'll start feeling fulfilled because you can look back and positively reflect on the meaning you've created for yourself over time. When you do that, you will feel a certain glow – which we often refer to as happiness.'

The man said,

'I understand. I'll start looking deeply and paying better attention. When I do something, and it sends that special feeling of energy through me, I will notice. Then, I will be sure to do it often. I will remember to live – not just exist – by doing what makes me feel alive.'

I replied,

'I'm glad you understand.'

The man responded,

'Thank you for your answers. They've helped me think about my life in a profound way, where I feel like much is possible, and I have the power to make it happen.'

I replied,

'Oh, it's been no trouble at all. I'm simply doing what makes me feel more alive.'

'Most people confuse the meaning of life with meaning in life.'

Professor
PETER ADAMSON

PROFESSOR PETER ADAMSON is an American philosopher and intellectual historian. He holds two academic positions: professor of philosophy in late antiquity and in the Islamic world at the Ludwig Maximilian University of Munich; and professor of ancient and medieval philosophy at King's College London. Adamson hosts the weekly podcast *History of Philosophy without any gaps*, which attempts to make accessible the history of philosophy in all cultures. Adamson has turned the podcast into an eponymous book series, and his latest book is *Don't Think for Yourself: Authority and Belief in Medieval Philosophy* (2022).

AS A HISTORIAN OF PHILOSOPHY, I am more qualified to speak about what thinkers of the past considered to be the 'meaning of life'.

Actually though, and perhaps contrary to expectations, this is not really a topic that comes up a lot in the history of philosophy. I can't think of a pre-modern text that speaks in so many words of the 'meaning of life', which is perhaps no bad thing since it is less than clear that life is the sort of thing that could have a 'meaning'. After all a person's life, or life itself, is not very much like a word or a sentence.

What we do find very frequently is the similar idea that life has a 'purpose', and maybe that's all that people have in mind when they talk about the meaning of life. What then is the 'purpose' of life? Well, Aristotle notes early in his *Nicomachean Ethics* that it is just obvious that the purpose of life is happiness; the tricky question, to his mind, is what happiness would consist in. He goes on to argue that the happy life is the one in which reason is used well, both in practical contexts (which means acting virtuously) and intellectual contexts (which means being a scientist or philosopher – for him these were the same thing).

Other ancient thinkers argued that happiness lies in pleasure; this is what we find in the Epicureans for example. It's striking, and often noted, that other ancient ethical traditions also seem to prioritize the happiness of the individual. Confucianism and Buddhism are good examples. The fact that this approach was widespread and appeared in several independent historical traditions might suggest that, as Aristotle said, it is just obvious that the purpose of life is to be happy. But not everyone would agree.

Some modern-day ethicists would say that the purpose of life is to maximize beneficial outcomes for everyone (all humans, or maybe even all sentient beings, so including animals). We tend to assume that this approach is a pretty recent one, and goes back to Utilitarians like Mill and Bentham, but we do actually find such a position in ancient China, in the Mohist school.

As for myself, I suppose I have found meaning or purpose in life partially by learning what historical philosophers have had to say about this and other deep questions. I'm not saying it is the purpose that everyone should adopt, but it works for me.

'I can't think of a pre-modern text that speaks in so many words of the "meaning of life".'

MELISSA STERRY

MELISSA STERRY is a transdisciplinary design scientist and complex systems theorist recognised as a world-leading authority on the science, technology, design and thinking that could help humanity to build a better world. Primarily working with projects that chart unprecedented conceptual, creative and commercial potentialities, including several first-to-market start-ups, Sterry has extensive experience of working with leading-edge ideas, individuals and institutions worldwide.

THE YEAR WAS 1990. A teenager, I was swimming, some distance out, in Maya Bay, the Phi Phi Islands, Thailand. An idyllic scene, I was enjoying the beauty of the crystal clear ocean, as it sparkled in the sunshine, and feeling not a care in the world. Then, without warning, I felt a searing stinging sensation across my thighs. My first thought was that I must have swum into discarded fishing gear. But, upon looking about me, there was neither line nor net. The penny then dropped. I'd been stung by a jellyfish. I knew it best not to panic, so I bit my lip, mustered Dutch courage, and swam back to shore. Upon walking out of the water I could see red welts rising across both legs, and called out for help. Of the fifteen or so people on the beach one was a diver who ran to give assistance. Looking over the welts he said it was impossible to tell the species: my guess was as good as his as to whether the sting was innocuous or lethal. If the latter, I'd be dead long before we reached medical assistance. Or indeed, even a painkiller. Perhaps, had the setting been different it would have been harder for me to embrace a state of calm. However, much aware that I was most fortunate that, if I was going to go I was going to go in paradise, I concluded to savour whatever time I had left. So, I breathed deeply, did all that I could do to alleviate the pain, which was to wash the welts with seawater, and, for as far as I could see, took in the sublime views about me.

Over the years that have since passed, there have been many moments when I have found myself unexpectedly confronted with difficult, and at times upsetting, situations. In each instance, if not immediately, within a period of days, I have immersed myself in a natural setting, because as in

Maya Bay in 1990, I find that when the many distractions of the human world are removed I can both think calmly, clearly and deeply, and I can feel connected to a bigger whole: to the ebb and the flow of life on Earth. Meaning, for me, comes in making the connections between one thing and another, such that, over time, I have built a sense of the workings of the world, and where I fit in those workings. Put succinctly, meaning, for me comes with having a sense of place – of my place within space and within time – no matter how mind-bogglingly vast those dimensions might be, and no matter the events taking place within them.

'Meaning, for me comes with having a sense of place – of my place within space and within time.'

MARK
STEVENSON

MARK STEVENSON is a strategic adviser to governments, investors and NGOs, and co-founder of carbon removals company CUR8. Working as a futurist, he helps organisations change the way they feel, think, invest and operate in order to answer the intertwined questions the future is asking us – on climate change, inequality, the retreat of democracy and the failures of the markets to price risk properly. His two best-selling books, *An Optimist's Tour of the Future* and the award-winning *We Do Things Differently*, map out some existing and proven solutions to our current dilemmas. He also co-presents the successful podcast *Jon Richardson and the Futurenauts*.

DANIEL DENNETT SAYS THAT ONE of the occupational hazards of being a philosopher is getting asked difficult questions at parties. Being solicited over drinks for free advice is, of course, commonplace. If you're a doctor you'll be asked to pass opinion on a dodgy knee. Financial types are regularly probed for investing tips. As an occasional writer I have often been asked to comment on 'this great idea for a book/play/sitcom I've come up with' and/or make an introduction to my literary agent. But if you're a philosopher it's worse. As you reach for another beer you might be asked something really quite tricky: 'What is consciousness?', 'Does free will exist?', 'Why Jeremy Clarkson?' Another recurring question philosophers are likely to be confronted with is, 'What's the definition of happiness?' Luckily Daniel says he's got an answer to that one, and it's a goodie: 'Find something more important than you are and dedicate your life to it.'

This is where I believe one can find what meaning there is to be had in life. For me, it is the bedrock upon which nearly everything else rests. I'm lucky enough to have found several 'bigger than me' things to have a crack at – battling climate change, facing down cynicism, making people laugh (and using comedy as a sharp tool in the search for truth), being a partner and parent, attempting to deliver the definitive prog-rock album. None of these are solo endeavours and necessitate collaboration with other 'bigger than me' types who are invariably the kindest and most interesting people to be around (and I have made something of a habit of working with collaborators who are all better than me – my beloved being the most extraordinary example). They stand in sharp contrast to those who only have projects the same size as (or smaller than) themselves, who are invariably tedious company, seeming capable only of talking about their kitchen extension, what they did on holiday and their plans for retirement – the 'walking corporate dead' as I like to call them (silently, in my head of course).

It is in my relationships with those other 'bigger than me' types in which I find the meaning that comes from being a social animal – the laughter, the communion, the shared challenge and enterprise of living for a brief moment on this most extraordinary and kind spaceship called Planet Earth.

My most recent friend has also contributed an answer for this book, the wonderful Tim Smit. Upon meeting him I realised he understood something else important about finding meaning in this world – and that is to take playfulness seriously.

I worry that all this sounds a little too obvious and painless. But it is not. When you lose the 'bigger than me', as we all do (and I have) there is an uncountable cost: the distance from your partner or children, the isolation from yourself (whilst simultaneously the stoking of the ego), the confusion and sadness of your peers, and the squandering of the only currency: time. The brutality of your own self-involvement can destroy meaning as surely as sunshine melts ice-cream.

What a gift then, to be asked by James Bailey to spend a moment thinking on this topic. Writing this brought me meaning.

Thank you James.

'Writing this brought me meaning.'

JOSHUA FLETCHER

JOSHUA FLETCHER, also known as Anxiety Josh, is an anxiety expert and psychotherapist. Having been diagnosed with several anxiety conditions, he combines his professional knowledge with lived experience to educate and help others. He has written three best-selling books that focus on self-help for anxiety, including *And How Does That Make You Feel?*.

THANK YOU FOR REACHING OUT with your question; it provided a welcome break in my busy week. Your inquiry taps into philosophical territory, which for me drew my attention to existentialist thinkers like Jean-Paul Sartre, Nietzsche and Heidegger. These philosophers, who have greatly influenced my thinking, suggest that we craft our own life's meaning, adhering to the idea that our existence comes before our essence. This notion resonates with me, especially Nietzsche's emphasis on the journey of becoming who we are through self-creation.

My personal quest for meaning has not been straightforward. Having faced significant losses early in life, including the passing of my little brother and father, and developing a crippling anxiety disorder, I've grappled with nihilistic feelings and a search for purpose. These experiences propelled me into exploring the meaning of life during moments when I felt most lost.

Today, as a therapist and author, I attribute my growth and success to the lessons learned from overcoming such profound grief. To me, life's essence is perpetual learning. Regardless of life's length, there's always something new to discover. This learning could be academic, or it could stem from the myriad lessons life throws our way. It's up to us to define our purpose, whether by adopting an existing framework or crafting our own, even though the latter might be more daunting.

I've found my purpose in helping others, which, I've realized, also helps me heal and grow. Living in alignment with my evolving values brings fulfillment, underscoring the importance of constant self-reflection and adaptation.

I cherish your question as it prompts further reflection and learning on my part. Thank you for the opportunity to share my thoughts.

GRETCHEN RUBIN

GRETCHEN RUBIN is one of today's most influential and thought-provoking observers of happiness and human nature. She's the author of many best-selling books, such as *The Happiness Project*, *Better than Before*, and *The Four Tendencies*, which have sold millions of copies in more than thirty languages. She's also host of the popular podcast *Happier with Gretchen Rubin*, and founder of the award-winning Happier app, which helps people track their happiness-boosting habits.

IN MY STUDY OF HAPPINESS and human nature, and in my own experiences, I found that the meaning of life comes through love. In the end, it is love – all kinds of love – that makes meaning.

In my own life, I find meaning, purpose and fulfilment by connecting to other people – my family, my friends, my community, the world. In some cases, I make these connections face-to-face, and others, I do it through reading. Reading is my cubicle and my treehouse; reading allows me better to understand both myself and other people.

'In the end, it is love – all kinds of love – that makes meaning.'

CHARLES DUHIGG

CHARLES DUHIGG is a Pulitzer prize-winning reporter and the author of *The Power of Habit*, which spent over three years on the *New York Times* best-seller lists. *Smarter Faster Better* and his latest book, *Supercommunicators*, have also been best-sellers. Duhigg has received the George Polk Award, the Gerald Loeb Award, the Investigative Reporters and Editors Medal, the Scripps Howard National Journalism Award and the Robert F. Kennedy Journalism Award. He currently writes for the *New Yorker* magazine.

WHAT IS THE MEANING OF LIFE?

I can honestly say:

I have no idea.

But I write this in London, where I am visiting with my wife and two boys. And they are healthy, and safe, and (mostly) happy, and there's joy in watching their delights: A clothing stall with a jacket they've long wanted; the way the double decker bus carries us above the fray; a monument to scientific discoveries beside a flower garden and goats.

I'm surrounded by evidence – of the Blitz, D-Day, colonies despoiled, JFK and MLK and 9/11 – that all could be otherwise. I hear about bombs falling on innocents, an uncertain election, a faltering climate, and many of us lacking the will (or charity) to change.

And yet, still, I marvel that we flew here in under 12 hours – while my ancestors required months and tragedies to transit in reverse – and I will send this note simply by hitting a button, and we can love whomever we want, and see and speak to them at any hour, and a pandemic did not end my life, did not kill my children's dreams, did not make society selfish and cruel.

And, for now, that's enough. I do not need to know the meaning of life. I do not need to know the purpose of it all. Simply breathing while healthy, and safe, and (mostly) happy, is such a surprising, awe-inducing, humbling gift that I have no right to question it. I won't tempt fate. I won't look that gift horse in the mouth. I'll simply hope my good fortune continues, work hard to share it with others, and pray I will remember this day, this moment, if my luck fades.

ROXIE NAFOUSI

ROXIE NAFOUSI is a self-development coach, inspirational speaker, manifesting expert and three-times *Sunday Times* best-selling author. She has been labelled 'the manifesting queen' by Forbes and the *Financial Times*, and her debut book, *MANIFEST: 7 Steps to Living Your Best Life*, has become a global success. After years of living a hedonistic lifestyle in her early twenties, fuelled by partying, addiction and poor self-care, Nafousi found herself at rock bottom. Then, in 2018, she heard about the term 'manifesting' and so began her inward journey to recovery and happiness.

WHAT THE FUCK IS IT ALL FOR? It's a question I've asked myself in my darkest times. Or when I've started pondering with awe and wonder at the magnitude of the universe and its infinite galaxies. To me, the meaning of life is about growing. It's about evolving, both personally and collectively. It's about experiencing true joy, love and happiness. It is about being present and grounded in the human experience and all its complexities. It's about facing challenges and learning from them. It's about having fun. It's about helping others. It's about being a part of something greater than yourself. It's about finding your purpose and using it to serve humanity.

'The meaning of life is about growing ... personally and collectively.'

MATT RIDLEY

MATT RIDLEY, The Viscount Ridley, DL, is a British science writer, journalist and businessman whose books have sold over a million copies. These include *The Red Queen*, *The Origins of Virtue*, *Genome*, *Nature via Nurture*, *Francis Crick*, *The Rational Optimist*, *The Evolution of Everything* and *How Innovation Works*. He also writes a weekly column in *The Times* and writes regularly for the *Wall Street Journal*. As Viscount Ridley, he was elected to the House of Lords in February 2013. He served on the Select Committee on Science and Technology 2014–2017.

THANK YOU FOR YOUR LETTER. Here's my answer:

There never has been and never will be a scientific discovery as surprising, unexpected and significant as that which happened on 28 February 1953 in Cambridge when James Watson and Francis Crick found the double-helix structure of DNA and realised that the secret of life is actually a very simple thing: it's infinite possibilities of information spelled out in a four-letter alphabet in a form that copies itself.

Matt

'The secret of life is actually a very simple thing.'

ADAM GRANT

ADAM GRANT is an organisational psychologist and #1 *New York Times* best-selling author of five books. He has been recognised as one of the world's ten most influential management thinkers, writes on work and psychology for the *New York Times*, has served on the Defense Innovation Board at the Pentagon, and has been honoured as a Young Global Leader by the World Economic Forum. He also hosts the TED podcasts *ReThinking* and *WorkLife*, which have been downloaded over sixty-five million times.

ON SABBATICAL, so sorry to be brief, but if there's an answer other than 42, I'd say it's this:

The meaning of life is to make other lives more meaningful.

Cheers,

Adam

'The meaning
of life is to
make other
lives more
meaningful.'

CHARLES SALVADOR

Prisoners

CHARLES SALVADOR

MICHAEL GORDON PETERSON, better known as Charles Bronson / Charles Salvador, is one of the UK's longest-serving prisoners, and was the subject of the 2008 biopic film *Bronson* starring Tom Hardy. First arrested as a petty criminal, he was convicted and sentenced in 1974 to seven years' imprisonment for armed robbery. Additional time was added due to attacks on prisoners and guards. Upon his release in 1987, he began a bare-knuckle boxing career in the East End of London. His promoter thought he needed a more suitable name and suggested he change it to Charles Bronson, after the American actor. He was returned to prison in 1988 after being convicted of planning another robbery. In 2014, he changed his name again, this time to Charles Salvador, in a mark of respect to Salvador Dalí, one of his favourite artists. The Charles Salvador Art Foundation was founded to promote his artwork and 'help those in positions even less fortunate than his own' to participate in art.

James *

Life is to Me A Gift.
You Have to Respect it.
   Appreciate it.
Hold on to it For As Long As Possible.

People Who Let go Dont Deserve it..

4½ Decades of My Life Have Been in a Hole.
   But Ive Still enjoyed it.

I Made it Work For Me.

Cuz I Found "Myself"

2v17
Best Wishes!

SALVADOR 1314. HMP. Wakefield. CAge

JAMES,

Life is to me a gift.

You have to respect it.

Appreciate it.

Hold on to it for as long as possible.

People who let go don't deserve it.

4½ decades of my life have been in a hole but I've still enjoyed it.

I made it work for me.

Coz I found 'myself'.

[Overleaf]Never piss on a rattle snake!

'4½ decades of my life have been in a hole but I've still enjoyed it.'

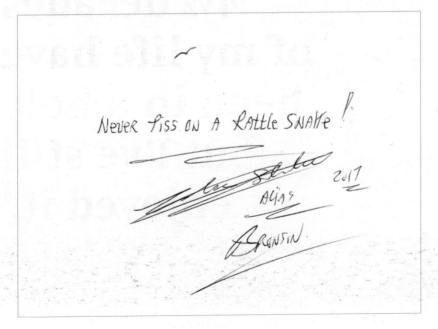

*What do you think is the **MEANING OF LIFE?***
How do you find meaning, purpose and fulfilment
in your own life?

_____

_____

_____

_____

_____

_____

_____

_____

_____

_____

_____

_____

_____

Acknowledgements

Thank you to my agent, Hannah Ferguson, for being by my side throughout the ups and downs of the publication journey. We finally got this book published!

A special thanks to my brilliant editor, Tamsin English, whose humour, honesty and support kept me sane (and laughing).

Shoutouts also to Emma Smith for believing in the book and to Sarah Thomas, Amanda Keats and Clare Sivell for all your hard work on it.

Over the years, I've been fortunate to receive assistance and encouragement from many amazing people, including Ava Eldred, Sophie O'Mahony, Richard Fu and Tim Bailey.

As ever, an enormous thank you to Mum and Dad for always being there (and for opening my post when I was away!). To Elizaveta for listening to countless hours of me rambling about this project: your love, support and unwavering belief in me mean the world. And to Rebecca – I think I can now officially declare myself the letter-writing champion!

And finally, to the wonderful contributors who generously shared personal stories and insights, I am eternally grateful. Your kindness, wisdom and willingness to open up to a complete stranger have made this book possible. Your thoughts sincerely helped me and will undoubtedly inspire readers for years to come.